THE FIRSTS
OF
AMERICAN JEWISH HISTORY
1492–1951
(FAMOUS FIRST FACTS FROM AMERICAN JEWISH HISTORY)

Christopher Columbus and Abraham Zacuto

The Firsts

of

American Jewish History

1492 - 1951

by

Tina Levitan, A.B.

Author of *"Haolam Hechadash"*,
the American Jewish History Series
in Hebrew

THE CHARUTH PRESS • BROOKLYN, NEW YORK

THIS BOOK IS AFFECTIONATELY DEDICATED
TO MY BELOVED PARENTS
BELLA AND JULIUS LEVITAN
WHOSE LOVE AND GUIDANCE HAVE BEEN THE
MAJOR INSPIRATION IN MY WRITING

PREFACE

This is a book of American Jewish historical beginnings; of first times, first places, first people, first things, and first institutions. This book and the pictures in it are about the contribution of the Jew to the growth of America.

Jews have lived in America since its discovery by Columbus. The contributions of Jewish voyagers and scientists were indispensable to Columbus in planning his expedition. In Columbus' crew, the first man to step ashore in the New World was a man of Jewish origin. And down through the history of our country Jewish people have been among the "first" to settle a newly discovered continent, to build cities, develop trade, found new industries, advance science, philanthropy, economic ideals, or to pursue a cultural life.

To fulfill this role of explorer, statesman, scientist, soldier, businessman or whatever it may be, takes courage, wisdom, imagination and backbreaking toil.

There may have been great Jews in America. Louis Dembitz Brandeis, the first Jew to be appointed to the United States Supreme Court was one; a wise man, a just man, a man who worked for the public good. There have been other Jews before and since, whose names are well known, but neither they nor Brandeis could have done their work without the help of the people whose names are forgotten: the ordinary, sensible, hardworking, humble men and women. The America they helped build has always been loved by its citizens.

Only those "Jewish Firsts" for which definate records are available are included here. Even in the most prosaic cases, historians often disagree as to the time, place, and participation of events. Counterclaims exist in almost every field because of the lack of authentic records and the unattainable testimony of the trail blazers, the discoverers, or whatever the case may be. It is possible that further research into unpublished records may reveal additional data. As more "American Jewish Firsts" are brought to light by historians, the author will appreciate having them called to her attention, with the hope of enlarging this body of information in subsequent editions of "The Firsts of American Jewish History."

The author desires to express her appreciation to the many historians, clergymen, librarians, chambers of commerce, government agencies, museums, scientific specialists and technicians who so generously cooperated in supplying and verifying the data herein presented.

It is hoped that this book will prove valuable for general reading and for reference and that it will inspire many to become interested in American Jewish history and look forward to the Tercentenary celebration of the landing of the Jews in 1654 in what is now New York.

Tina Levitan

Brooklyn, N.Y.
February 1, 1952

TABLE OF CONTENTS

LIST OF ILLUSTRATIONS

Permission to use the illustrations was graciously extended by the following:

AMERICAN JEWISH HISTORICAL SOCIETY
MUSEUM OF THE CITY OF NEW YORK
THE NEW YORK PUBLIC LIBRARY
MOUNT SINAI HOSPITAL
CONGREGATION SHEARITH ISRAEL
YESHIVA COLLEGE
HADASSAH

XV

1. THE FIRST JEW IN AMERICA

The story of the Jews in the building of America starts in the year 1492. Up to that time in Spain for hundreds of years the Jews had lived in what is still remembered as the Golden Age. They had produced philosophers, scientists, scholars, musicians, and poets. They helped make Spain famous for learning and culture. But in 1492 Ferdinand, the king of Spain, culminated a long succession of persecution by ordering the Jews to renounce their religion or leave Spain. The inhuman Inquisition was set up and many Jews in order to conceal their identity to escape death accepted Christianity and became known as Marranos. Many more chose to remain Jews and went into exile.

On Friday, August 3, 1492, a little before sunrise, the day after the expulsion of the Jews from Spain, Columbus, with the sails of his three ships puffed out, started on his great journey. His voyage was financed by a number of Marranos. Among these were Luis de Santangel, Chancellor of the royal Spanish household, Abraham Senior, Gabriel Sanchez, and Don Isaac Abravanel. He had also received much information from Jewish voyagers and scientists including Judah Cresques, the "map Jew" who headed a school of navigation, Abraham Zacuto, astronomer, and Levi ben Gershon, inventor of nautical instruments. He took with him on his trip at least five Marranos, Rodrigo de Triana, who was the first to see land, Alfonso de la Calle, Marco, the surgeon, Bernal, the fleet's physician, and Luis de Torres, the interpreter, the one who was to be the first to step upon American soil.

Finally after three months of traveling, on a sunny autumn day, on October 12, 1492, on the Jewish festival of Hoshannah Rabbah, Columbus and his crew came to San Salvador, the first little island to be reached by them. When land was sighted, Luis De Torres, a man of great learning, who could speak Hebrew, Arabic, and several other Asiatic languages, was sent ahead by Columbus and asked to head the first inland expedition of any kind undertaken by white men in America. After traveling twelve miles into the interior of the mainland, now know as Cuba, in search of the capital city of the Great Khan

1

of Tartary which De Torres was expected to find, much to his amazement, he discovered a town containing fifty straw huts built in the manner of tents. It was inhabited by about a thousand dark-skinned half-naked men and women who spoke a tongue not known to the white man. However, De Torres, making himself understood by gestures and sign language soon gained their friendship. The natives were so delighted with him that they brought cotton, ornaments, and live parrots to trade.

De Torres returned to Columbus with a lively and accurate description of everything he saw and gave his account of the natives smoking tobacco. Later he was the first white man to introduce its use into the Old World. He was overcome by the magnificent, heavy-laden fruit trees, beautiful flowers, and balmy climate of the island and persuaded Columbus to allow him to settle there. He was awarded a grant of land and human slaves by an Indian chieftain whose friendship he won, and with a pension granted him by King Ferdinand, he built himself a house. Here he had fine gardens, and meadows, began to grow tobacco and traded with the Indians.

De Torres lost no time in inviting his coreligionists to come and join him in the New World that was free from religious persecutions and in the same Hebrew letter to his old home, was the first to give the great American bird, the turkey, its name, calling it "tukki" from the Hebrew word for "peacock".

The first white man and first member of his race to settle in Cuba, he lived a peaceful and honorable life there, and was a symbol of the great need for freedom and security of the Spanish Jews who came to these shores, and of the bold pioneering spirit of those that followed him.

2.   THE FIRST BOOK OF IMPORTANCE PUBLISHED IN NORTH AMERICA

The Pilgrim Fathers who founded Plymouth, the first English colony in North America, were a Bible loving people. Although they did not know many Jewish people personally, the Bible was their guide and Moses their lawgiver. When they drew up a code to govern themselves, they followed the code of laws which Moses had given to the Jews. In their struggles for religious freedom, the Pilgrims liked to compare themselves with the Hebrews whom Moses had led from the slavery of Egypt to the freedom of Canaan. Following the model they found in the Bible, they planned their own Thanksgiving.

It is not surprising then to find that the first triumph of the American press should be Biblically inspired. The first book of importance published in North America was the "Bay Psalm Book" originally called "The Whole Book of Psalms, Faithfully Translated Into English Metre."

In 1636, several New England divines including Richard Mather, John Eliot and Thomas Welde undertook the work of translating the Psalms from the original Hebrew, a job that was completed in the summer of 1638. In 1640 an edition of 1,700 copies was printed at a cost of 33 pounds by the first printing establishment to be set up in English America which was located in Cambridge, Massachusetts in the house of President Dunster, the first president of Harvard College. The new Psalm Book was immediately adopted by nearly every congregation in the Massachusetts Bay Colony and was a notable achievement of the time. Fittingly enough there are to be found in it several Hebrew words as well as the Hebrew alphabet, the letters of which all bear the earmarks of local American workmanship.

In the top rank of the world's most famous books, the "Bay Psalm Book" is considered far rarer than a Shakespeare First Folio and can be compared in rarity and value to the Gutenberg Bible.

The highest amount ever paid for a book in auction — $151,000 was attained by the celebrated "Bay Psalm Book" on January 28, 1948 when it was sold at auction at the Parke-Bernet Galleries in New York.

The auctioned book known as the Crowninshield-Stevens-Brinley-Vanderbuilt-Whitney copy, is one of eleven copies known to exist, and one of four in private hands.

The first complete Hebrew edition of the Book of Psalms was published in this country in Cambridge, Massachusetts in 1809 and is believed to be the first Hebrew publication of this kind in America.

The first book to be published in North America by Jews appeared in 1760 and was written in English. It consisted of "The Form of Prayer Which Was Performed at the Jews' Synagogue in the City of New York on Thursday, October 23, 1760" and was so entitled. A more complete High Holiday prayer book appeared in English in 1766 and was made necessary, as the author, Isaac Pinto explains in his preface, "because in the British Dominions in America our brethren could best understand our prayers . . . in the language of the country wherein it hath pleased the Divine Providence to appoint his lot."

3.   THE FIRST HEBREW AUTHOR IN AMERICA

Prior to the coming of the Jews to North America, the record is replete with cases of Jewish settlement in South America, the earliest Jewish settlers going to that section of the country that first was settled. It was not, however, until 1642, that the first organized Jewish community in America came into existence. The Dutch had captured Recife, the capital of Brazil, and had driven out the Spanish rulers who brought the Inquisition with them to the New World. Many secret Jews living there and in other parts of South America took advantage of Holland's liberal policy by gradually settling there and openly returning to Judaism. The settlement increased rapidly from every source until with the arrival of six hundred people from Holland it contained about five thousand people.

So successful were these first Jewish settlers of Brazil in introducing the cultivation and manufacture of sugar into that country, that they decided that they could afford a professional rabbi to be their spiritual leader and direct the education of their children. Rabbi Isaac Aboab de Fonseca, a good Talmudic scholar and said to have been an excellent speaker, was summoned from Amsterdam. He organized the first congregation in America which was called "Kahal Kodesh" or "The Holy Congregation". Although he returned to Holland in a few years, he is the earliest American rabbi and also has the distinct honor of being the first Hebrew author in America.

His first publication appeared in 1649 at which time he translated the Bible into Portuguese and translated into Hebrew
two books dealing with mystic lore, one called "Beth Elohim"
or "The House of God," and the other "Shaar Shamaim" or
"The Gates of Heaven." The former was originally published
in Venice in 1576. The first edition in its original leather bind-
ing was acquired in 1947 by the Boston Hebrew Teachers' College
from the private collection of Rabbi Emanuel Eckstein of Cleveland, where it is carefully being studied, cherished and preserved for the future.

Rabbi Aboab was also the author of the first Hebrew poem
written on American soil, the original manuscript of which may
be seen in the library of the Theological Seminary in Amsterdam. It is entitled "Zecher Rab" or "The Great Remembrance"
which described the sufferings of the Jews due to their loyalties
to their Dutch rulers in the war that broke out with the Portuguese. Just as prosperity and freedom seemed assured and the
future seemed most rosy, the Portuguese laid seige to Recife.
Many of the Jewish immigrants were killed by the enemy and
died of starvation. Those who could, escaped, some going back
to Europe, others to the West Indies and North America. Thus
the first work written by a Jew in America was the history of
suffering, related in verse.

4. THE FIRST JEWISH SETTLER IN NEW AMSTERDAM

Although here and there are records of possible Jews in other
colonies at an early date, Jacob Barsimson of Holland who came
as one of a party of emigrants sent by the Dutch West India
Company to help populate its new colony in New Amsterdam —
as the Dutch called New York, seems to have the honor of
being the first Jewish settler in what is now the United States.
He came to New Amsterdam directly from Holland on the ship
"Peartree" as early as August 22, 1654, a month ahead of a
larger group of Jews.

New Amsterdam had been founded twenty-eight years before

by the Dutch West India Company which had Jewish stock-
holders and directors. It had gained a reputation as a fur trade
center and its excellent harbor was well-known. It was at the
insistance and encouragement of the Jews of Old Amsterdam
that Barsimson decided to settle in New Amsterdam.

He was alloted a weatherbeaten hut in the woods outside the
settlement where Indians once bartered furs for beads and
Peter Minuit had in 1628 bought Manhattan Island for 60 guild-
ers. For his neighbors, he found a mixed people who were still
celebrating with gay flags and bunting, the granting of a city
charter. He traded with the Indians, cleared land, planted gardens and orchards, and for a period of time hired himself out as
a manual laborer.

At the same time that Barsimson was disembarking at New
Amsterdam, a little ship the "St. Charles," after a narrow escape
from pirates, was making its slow uncertain way towards the
same port. Barsimson, together with these new arrivals were to
constitute the first Jewish community in North America which
was to have other "firsts" as well.

The first case in the colonies in which the observance of a
Jew for his Sabbath was recognized by the authorities as a
good reason for failure to attend court when summoned on that
day to appear, was brought against Barsimson in 1658. The
record reads: "Though the defendant is absent yet no default
is entered against him as he was summoned on his Sabbath."
What the case related to is not noted, and no further entry
appears.

5. THE FIRST JEWISH SETTLEMENT IN NORTH AMERICA

In September 1654, one month after Jacob Barsimson is
known to have settled in New Amsterdam, twenty-three poor
but healthy Jews also arrived to constitute there the first Jewish
settlement in North America. They came on the French bark
"St. Charles" from Recife, Brazil, where hoping to escape the
Portuguese invaders, some 600 Jews had boarded 50 different

vessels that were to take them back home to Holland across the sea. Ships headed for Holland had already undertaken their course, but the "St. Charles" had not gone very far when a storm arose, separating it from all the others. It drifted on the high seas only to be attacked by pirates who took the meager possessions of all those on board. Instead of landing in Holland, it finally reached New Amsterdam.

Although it was a pleasant change from the ship, the view of New Amsterdam which greeted the little group of Jews was not that of another London or Paris, but it compared favorably with Jamestown or Plymouth or the recently found village of Boston. There was the semblance of a hotel maintained by the Dutch West India Company, the owners of the colony, and the closing hours of the taverns were not turned into a day of penance. A considerable sum remained due to the captain of the "St. Charles," Jacques de la Motte, for their board and passage, and as the principal men among them had signed an agreement whereby they had become jointly and severally liable for the whole amount, very vigorous proceedings were taken against them. An auction sale was held of their goods and the proceeds being unable to discharge their indebtedness, two of the group, David Israel and Moses Ambrosius, were ordered to be taken into confinement and held until the amount was made up.

Peter Stuyvesant who ruled the colony at the time was angry to see the people trying to enter his little town and, lost no time in making his sentiments felt. At once he wrote a letter with his objections to Holland, but the newcomers wrote at the same time and were backed by the Dutch Jews. A reply was sent them in April, 1655, "They shall have permission to sail and trade in New Netherland, and to live and remain there, provided the poor poor among them shall not become a charge upon the deaconry or the company," it stated.

Within the ten years that Jews lived in New Amsterdam under Dutch rule, they progressed and established a firm foothold in that part of the world. They began as a small and insignificant group, but by the time of the English conquest, there were quite a number of wealthy tradesmen among them. The economic activities of the Jews of New Amsterdam were not very far reaching, but are interesting as the first ones made on the North American continent.

By the time the first constitution of the State of New York was adopted in 1777, Jews were put on an absolute equality with all other citizens, New York having been the first State actually granting full religious liberty.

6. THE FIRST CHAIR OF HEBREW AT AN AMERICAN COLLEGE

The first college founded in North America was Harvard College which began in 1636 only a few years after the first settlers came to Massachusetts. It was named for a young minister John Harvard who left the college his library and four hundred pounds when he died. During the first few decades after the founding of Harvard College, no course of study figured more largely than Hebrew. This was so because most of the students attending were preparing for the ministry. It was therefore required that they be able to read the Bible in its original language.

Originally Hebrew was taught by the president and the tutors along with the other undergraduate studies in the earliest years of the college. In 1655 one of the first of the endowed professorships — that of Hebrew and Oriental languages was established. Harvard students were required to spend one day each week for three years on Hebrew and allied tongues. The principal text used was the Bible. About twelve copies with the students inscriptions upon them from the years 1651 to 1746 are extant. Another text used was Wilhelm Schickards "Horologium Hebraeum" or the "Hebrew Sun Dial" which professed to teach the elements of the language in twenty-four hours. Following the Harvard pattern other colleges such as Yale, Columbia, Brown, Princeton, Johns Hopkins, as well as the University of Pennsylvania also taught Hebrew from their inception and have been teaching it to this day.

The first Hebrew Grammar published in America was written

in 1735 by Judah Monis, the first Jew to receive a college degree in America as well as the only Jew to receive a Harvard degree before 1800. But he did not remain a Jew for long, for in 1722 — less than two years later — he was baptized in the college hall. The following month he was appointed instructor of Hebrew at Harvard, but it is open to question whether Monis would have obtained this position if he would not have joined their Congregational Church. He took charge of all the Hebrew classes and began dictating his Grammar, to be copied in longhand by his students, until he was given a grant by the college to publish it in 1735 under the title of "Dickdook Leshon Gnebreet." Type was imported from England, but arrived in an imperfect condition, and had to be completed by a later shipment. When finally finished Monis' Grammar constituted the first complete Hebrew book published in America.

The influence of the Hebrew culture went far beyond the bounds of technical scholarship and professional training for theologians. This influence has permeated and colored the thought and feeling of this nation ever since its beginning.

The influence of the Hebrew language has found its way into American speech. About half the verses of the "Book of Psalms" have virtually become English idioms. Almost all the phrases of "Proverbs," "Job," "Song of Songs," "Ecclesiastes," and others have been domesticated by the English speaking peoples. Hebrew words like bath, bedlam, jug, mobile, cherub, seraph, sack, and vermillion, have become part of the English vernacular. Cities with Hebrew names or Hebrew derivatives can be found in every part of the United States. Thus we have, Sharon, Mass., New Canaan, Conn., Bethleham, N. H., Hebron, Calif., Giload, La., and Joseph, Idaho, to mention but a few.

7. THE FIRST JEWISH CONGREGATION IN NORTH AMERICA

Soon after they landed at New Amsterdam, as New York was then called, the early Jewish settlers, following the Orthodox Sephardic ritual, as early as 1655 formed a congregation

and organized under the name of Congregation Shearith Israel
or "Remnant of Israel." By a law of February 1, 1656, no type
of religious assembly was permissable, except family prayers,
outside the confines of the established Church. Even the Dutch
Lutherans had been unable to break through the vested privilege of the Dutch Reformed Church, the prevailing one, in
religious matters. Therefore from the start it was useless for
the Jews to hope for the fight to conduct public worship in
their own quarters.

But the Jews tried. At first they held services under the
branches of friendly trees, and then in private homes. We do not
know the exact date when the legal impediment to the establishment of a synagogue was removed; but evidence exists to show
that, before the end of the seventeenth century, in 1682, a house,
rented for the purpose, was used by the Congregation as a
place of public worship. The house, a small, rough, one story
and one room building, not very different from the homes of the
settlers or the churches of their neighbors of which there
were a total number of six in New York County, was located
on what is now called Beaver Street, between Broadway and
Broad Street.

In 1728 the little congregation which had grown to twenty
families, out of a total population of eight hundred and fifty-five
families living in New York at the time, was ready to build a
house of worship of their own. After preliminary preparations,
by September 8, 1729, the foundation stone of the first regular
synagogue in North America was laid on Mill Street, where a
mill then stood. The building was finally completed on April 18,
1730, and remained in use for almost a century. Originally a
little stone building with a fence around it, it stood at the
present site of South William Street where the great banks and
office buildings of today contain nothing to remind us of the
pioneer Jews of those early days.

Luiz Gomez, a New York merchant who achieved an enviable
position in the export of wheat, gave the synagogue a liberal
contribution to its support, and was elected its first president.
Mrs. Abigail Franks then founded the first Jewish sisterhood and
purchased the Holy Ark, the Menorah, and the Scrolls for the
congregation. To this day on every Yom Kippur, the Shearith

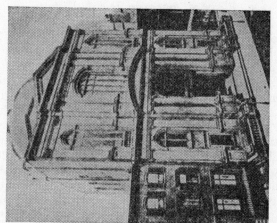

Shearith Israel's Nineteenth Street Synagogue—1860-1897

The Mill Street Synagogue 1730-1817

11

Israel recalls her soul in prayer during the Memorial Services, in grateful memory of her many pious deeds for the welfare of the congregation.

The first chazzan or reader of services was Saul Brown, one of the merchants who had been admitted to the burgher right in 1685. For his annual salary he received fifty British pounds plus six cords of wood and a supply of matzos for his family. The shamash or helper received a salary of sixteen pounds plus two cords of wood and a supply of matzos as well. The Reverent Gershom Mendez Seixas, the patriot-rabbi of the American Revolution, served as minister of this congregation for more than fifty years. During this time some of the most prominent Jewish merchants of colonial New York numbered among its members. (see Ch. 19).

Congregation Shearith Israel also known as the Spanish and Portuguese Synagogue still exists today and is the oldest continuous congregation in America and one of the oldest bodies of worship of any kind. It now flanks Central Park West at Seventieth Street in Manhattan and still observes the Orthodox Sephardic ritual as it did from the beginning.

The oldest synagogue building in America still in existence today is the Touro Synagogue which was built in 1763 in Newport, Rhode Island, site of the second Jewish settlement in North America. This solid looking structure which is still pleasing to the eye is an elegent example of colonial architecture and was recently designated as the first national shrine of Judaism in this country by the United States Government. (see Ch. 88).

The third Jewish congregation was established in Philadelphia in 1745, where Jews had resided since 1703. Savannah was the site where the Jews settled in Georgia in 1732. Their synagogue was built two years later. When Washington became president, he sent letters to all these synagogues which are often quoted today for the strength of their statements against all forms of intolerance.

8. THE FIRST JEWISH CEMETERY IN NORTH AMERICA

In July, 1655 when Abraham de Lucena, Salvador Dandrada, and Jacob Cohen, three of the original settlers who had come to New Amsterdam on the "St. Charles," petitioned the governor and directors of the colony for the right to establish a Jewish cemetery, they were told that they might have one when the need arose. There was a need the following year, for on July 14, 1656, one of the newcomers died, and a tract of land was set aside for them from the colony lands. The site was outside the village, north of Wall Street, where the Dutch had built the city wall, near the present location of Chatham Square on the New Bowery. During the Revolutionary War, the cemetery was fortified by the patriots as one of the defences of the city.

A small part of this cemetery with only a few tombstones bearing both Hebrew and Spanish inscriptions still exists today, although the stones that mark the graves are eroded so that many of the inscriptions are no longer legible and have almost been completely lost with the growth of the city. Among those known to have been buried here are fourteen Jewish soldiers who fought in the Revolutionary War including Simon Nathan who was a private in Captain Andrew Geyer's Third Company of the Philadelphia Militia who at the risk of his life supplied the Continental Forces with canvas and powder. Here also lies the Reverent Gershom Mendez Seixas, the minister of the Shearith Israel Congregation who closed his congregation when the Redcoats entered the city, and next to him his brother Benjamin Mendez Seizas, who served as a lieutenant in the New York Militia and who helped to found the New York Stock Exchange.

At annual Memorial Day exercises at the cemetery, the Asser Levy Garrison of the Army and Navy Union named after the hardly early American Jewish pioneer, decorates each of the graves with an American flag, and at the same time the Rabbi of the Shearith Israel Congregation recounts the deeds of the men who lay beneath the stones.

A tablet marking the remains of the cemetery, which is the oldest Jewish landmark in the United States, was erected in

1903 under the auspices of the "American Scenic and Historic Preservation Society" and the "American Jewish Historical Society." Two other sites located respectively on what is now West 11th Street, near Sixth Avenue, and on the south side of Twenty-first Street, a little to the west of Sixth Avenue, are similarly designated, the tablets being marked, second and third cemetery respectively.

The Jewish cemetery at Newport, Rhode Island, which was founded in 1677, is the oldest Jewish cemetery existing in its entirety today. Henry Wadsworth Longfellow, the poet, inspired by the tombstones bearing Hebrew and Spanish inscriptions, wrote a poem about the Newport cemetery entitled "The Jewish Cemetery at Newport" at a time when there were no Jews living in the city at all. Emma Lazarus, an American Jewish poetess of the same period to whose pen belong the glowing words of "The New Colossus" inscribed on the base of the Statue of Liberty, also wrote a poem about the cemetery entitled "The New Ezekiel."

9.   THE FIRST JEWISH SOLDIER IN NORTH AMERICA

The defense of New Amsterdam, the little Dutch settlement clustering on the tip of Manhattan Island, was in the hands of the colonists, the burghers, or citizen soldiers who had obtained such guns, pistols, and shot and powder as they could. The lurking Indians and marauding Swedes made no distinction between young or old, Jew or Christian. Following the custom established in Holland, Jews were excluded from military duty but were required to pay a tax which amounted to a dollar thirty a month.

In the New World the early Jewish settlers had hoped to reside in a country where they could stand up alongside their Christian neighbors and, with them, share the hazards of defense, as well as the responsibilities of peace. It was not before long that a handful of Jews under the leadership of Jacob Barsimson and Asser Levy Van Swellem, one of the original settlers who had come over on the "St. Charles," demanded and secured from the Dutch authorities the right to stand guard at the stockade of New Amsterdam. Although the request at first was refused time and again, the determined Levy mounted on guard duty and passed many a watchful hour peering into the wilderness.

On April 21, 1657, Asser Levy Van Swellem won another victory in which a principle was involved. Proving that he kept watch and ward like the other burghers of the city, he was admitted to the burgher right, paving the way for the right of citizenship for his people and other minority groups.

Thanks are also due to Levy and his associates for establishing the right of free trade throughout the colony. Levy, who for a while had sent himself up as a trader, appealed to the authorities in Holland who heeded his plea of keeping the trade open to all. Levy was also the first Jewish landowner in North America and owned the land on which was built the first synagogue. As early as 1661 he had purchased property in Albany and acquired a piece of land on South William Street. In 1660, he was licensed as butcher at a time when licenses were restricted to only six in the colony and occupied the first Jewish butcher shop which was located on Wall Street. The same year he built the first Jewish slaughterhouse in America so that "all persons should have the liberty to kill and hang therein meat."

At the time of his death in 1681, Levy was considered amongst the wealthiest inhabitants. His grounds and buildings were appraised at two hundred and eighteen pounds and the slaughterhouse which was located outside the city gates at eighteen hundred pounds.

No other Jew of his time seems to have had so many dealings with Christians as he did. He was named as the executor in the wills of many Christian merchants. He was always ready to defend Jewish as well as non-Jewish rights. In 1671 he lent money for the building of the first Lutheran Church in New York.

The name of Asser Levy Van Swellen stands out as that of a determined and of an admirable character whose life work made its small contribution to the upbuilding of the new continent.

10. THE FIRST JEWISH DOCTOR IN AMERICA

There were Spanish and Portuguese physicians of note who came to the New World at an early date and practiced medicine in Recife, the first Jewish settlement in Brazil. Dr. Jacob Lumbrozo, a Portuguese physician who arrived in Maryland on January 24, 1656, two years after the arrival of the first Jews in New Amsterdam, is North America's earliest Jewish physician. He was the first Jewish settler in Maryland and the only Jew there at the time. He built up a lucrative trade in Charles County where his arrival formed a distinct event in the life of the province. He imported a servant, began raising tobacco, became a county squire and for nearly a decade continued as an important figure in its economic activity.

Although the early proprietors of Maryland, the Calverts were Roman Catholics and intended the colony to be an asylum only for the persecuted members of their faith, Lumbrozo was not disturbed in the practice of his profession as a physician until 1658, when he was arrested and tried for being a nonconformist, in violation of the Act Concerning Religion which had become a law. The case was the only one of its kind brought against a Jew in the entire thirteen colonies. However, Lumbrozo was soon discharged under a general amnesty in honor of Richard Cromwell and acquired certain civil rights and a grant of land in 1663.

Following Lumbrozo's example practically every Jewish community after his time had its own physician. To inform the public of their presence, doctors would print announcements to the effect that they intended to practice the art of healing, and agreed to cure persons free of charge if they could show a certificate from a clergyman that they were really poor. Letters addressed to them were expected to be postpaid and those who lived at a distance and desired aid were requested to send a horse for transportation.

One of the most interesting of these early physicians, Dr. Sicarry, also a Portuguese Jew who settled in Virginia at the beginning of the eighteenth century was the first to introduce the tomato as an edible vegetable, which for a long time was considered poisonous and mostly used as a garden ornament.

Dr. Sicarry called tomatoes "apples" and he believed that a person who ate enough of these "apples" would never die. No one knows how many tomatoes Dr. Sicarry ate, but he lived to a very ripe old age.

11. THE FIRST JEWISH SCHOOL IN AMERICA

Long before the days of the free public school system throughout the nation the most interesting and significant means of education among the Jews were the congregational schools. True to the teachings of the Hebrew prophets—"and thou shalt teach thy children", each congregation conducted some kind of Jewish education and general school training as well.

The first of these schools was established in 1728, by the Congregation Shearith Israel, the same year in which was erected their first regular synagogue. Children came on foot or horseback from all over the island to sit on backless benches in a building adjacent to the synagogue which was used as a schoolhouse. In charge of education was the chazzan or reader and a special teacher, presumably, for the more secular subjects. In this early period, in keeping with the traditional outlook and practice of the Jews of Europe, Hebrew and allied subjects were the main ones taught.

In 1775, Shearith Israel opened one of the earliest schools combining secular and Hebrew education, a practice unheard of at that time in many countries. The school continued to exist until the Revolution, when most of the Jews left New York. The children were taught Spanish, English writing, arithmetic along with Hebrew. The hours of study were from nine to twelve in the winter and from two to five in the summer. Most of the day was devoted to Hebrew; English writing and arithmetic could not have taken more than an hour a day, and Spanish at the most, another hour. In 1762, the synagogue secured the services of Abraham Israel Abrahams, who was a professional teacher at a salary of twenty pounds a year for teaching the poor children. His income was supplemented by an eight pound fee paid by each of the wealthier students. The trustees of the school visited the school regularly in rotation.

In 1802 the Shearith Israel Congregational School was reorganized as the "Polonies Talmud Torah" and still exists today under that name as the oldest religious school in America. The regular day school pattern was continued until 1840 when it finally became limited to religious and Hebrew instruction only. As the public school system gradually developed, the congregational schools became supplementary, meeting on afternoons or on Sundays or both.

Rebecca Gratz, an outstanding Jewish woman, founded the first Sunday School in America in Philadelphia in 1838 and was its supervisor and president for twenty-six years. This Sunday School still exists today in Philadelphia where the home of the Protestant Sunday School movement began. Isaac Leeser, a rabbi and writer along Jewish lines, founded the Hebrew Education Association of that city in 1848. The Association organized a little school with twenty-two pupils which expanded bit by bit. It was the first religious school in America that met on afternoons and on Sunday. The Hebrew language, Bible and Jewish history were the subjects taught, and the school became known as the Talmud Torah.

Today the Talmud Torah's are still one of the chief kinds of Jewish schools in this country, by which Jewish children can learn about the great deeds of their people and their great religious heritage, although the Yeshiva, or all day parochial school movement which combines both secular and Hebrew subjects has shown a tremendous increase in enrollment throughout the country during the past decade.

12. THE FIRST JEWISH ARTIST IN AMERICA

Myer Myers, a silversmith who lived in New York in 1746 is America's first Jewish artist. For many years he was a member of the Congregation Shearith Israel. In 1786 he was elected president of the Silversmith's Society of New York. Several of his exquisite Chanukkah Lamps, spice boxes, ceremonial objects originally made for Shearith Israel and Jeshuat Israel in

A silver tankard showing the Livingston Family coat of arms made by Myer Myers, America's first Jewish artist

Newport, as well as a silver tankard showing the coat of arms of the Livingston family, still exist today. They all carry his trade mark, MM, which stands for his name.

His artistic craftsmanship and intricate workmanship produced pieces highly valued. Ironically, one of them found its way into the collection of the late Czar of Russia.

There is another early American Jewish artist who deserves mention, Joshua Cantir, the eighteenth century Jewish artist of Charleston, South Carolina. Another, perhaps America's third Jewish craftsman whose name has been preserved for us, is David Lopez, also of Charleston, South Carolina, who was the builder and architect of the present synagogue Kahal Kodesh Beth Elohim, the fourth oldest congregation in the United States, organized on the day following Rosh Hashanah in 1749 two score years before the birth of the United States.

13. THE FIRST JEWISH OFFICER IN AMERICA

Although lovers of peace from the days of Solomon and Jeremiah, Jews have fought in all the wars of this country with distinction and honor.

The first instance of Jewish participation in the armed forces is at the opening of the French and Indian War in 1754. Isaac Meyers of New York called a town meeting at the Rising Sun Inn and set up a company of soldiers of which he was chosen captain in the expedition across the Allegeheny Mountains.

There were other Jews who were alert to the growing dangers in the French and Indian campaigns and the names of Jewish soldiers appear in a record of the skirmishes and battles of the period. Men named Jacob Wolf and Jacob Wexler served in the ranks. Lieutenant Joseph Levy participated in the Cherokee uprising in South Carolina in 1761. A Captain Elias Meyer was a member of the Royal American Regiment whose recommendation for promotion stated that he was an engineer, probably America's first Jewish engineer of whom we have a record, and who had previously served as a lieutenant.

By the time the American movement for independence began,

a considerable number of Jews became officers in the Continental forces. The record shows at least four Jews as lieutenant-colonels, three as majors, and certainly six, probably more as captains.

Some of the better known officers include Lieutenant-Colonel David Salisbury Franks, who accompanied Arnold on his retreat from Canada and who afterwards fought on through the war, Colonel Isaac Franks, his cousin and Colonel Solomon Bush. In Georgia, Mordecai Sheftall became Deputy Commissioner-General of Issues (see Ch. 22). Major Benjamin Nones, often referred to as the Jewish Lafayette, came from France in 1777 and served on the staffs of both Washington and Lafayette and later was attached to the command of Baron de Kalb, in which there were a number of Jews. When De Kalb was fatally wounded in the thickest of the fighting in the Battle of Camden, the three to bear him from the field were Major Nones, Captain De La Motte and Captain Jacob De Leon, all Jews. Nones is the first Jewish major of whom we have a record. (see Ch. 24).

14. THE FIRST INDIGO PLANT IN AMERICA

Moses Lindo, a Portuguese Jew who came to Charleston, South Carolina in 1756 after having spent several years in England, introduced the indigo industry in the thirteen colonies. On his large plantation in Charleston, he established the first indigo plant in North America and invested some two hundred thousand pounds in the business. He is said to have learned about indigo production in London where he attended the Merchant Taylor's School and where for three years he obtained practical experience in the trade. He continued a correspondence with the dyers of the London Royal Society and was continually making new improvements in keeping with their findings. He even is said to have offered prizes to induce new methods of production.

"The Philosophical Transactions," a trade periodical of 1763 contains a letter of his which describes his discovery of a new dye made from pouck, a native week cooked in Bristol water.

Due to his pioneering efforts, a fabulous Carolina indigo trade developed which was responsible for the backbone of the wealth of the colony and he became its leading exporter and importer. It was his mark of inspection which qualified the Carolina grown product for acceptance in British markets. In recognition of his work in the field, he was appointed Surveyor and Inspector General of Indigo Dyes and Drugs for the Carolina provinces, and had the right of using the royal coat of arms of George III over his door.

The petition to appoint him inspector was signed by the lieutenant governor, council members, members of the assembly, merchants and planters. It stated that, "because of the services rendered to this province by Moses Lindo, and as testimonial of his abilities he be made public inspector," because "he is the only person known to us capable of rendering this province public service in that article."

In 1754 Charleston exported more than two hundred thousand pounds of indigo and the amount increased until it ranked second to rice.

After serving as Inspector General for ten years, Lindo resigned because he wrote, he could not bring himself to accept and certify inferior indigo.

Lindo was familiar with the practice of English universities in excluding Jews and was greatly impressed by the account of Brown University in Providence, Rhode Island with its atmosphere of tolerance and enlightment. He was the magnanimous donor of twenty pounds, one of the largest amounts ever given to the university up to that time. Brown already had a provision excusing attendence on the Sabbath, but following the acceptance of this gift, we find a resolution passed by the university which reads:

"Voted that the children of the Jews may be admitted into this institution and enjoy the freedom of their religion, without any restraint or imposition whatsoever."

15. THE FIRST JEWISH INTERCOLONIAL FURRIER

Alive to the rich potentialities of America, Jews in the early colonial days contributed their best effots in laying the economic foundations of the country. They furthered the whale and candle industry in New England, and grew indigo in the Carolinas. When the Non-Importation Resolutions of 1765 went into effect, from the very beginnings of the conflict between the colonists and the mother country, true to the teachings of their faith which is predominantly the faith of liberty, Jewish shippers turned to the fur trade, sending their trappers, hunters, and agents as far west as the Mississippi. These fur traders were amongst the first pioneers and colonizers, holding the country until the land-hungry settlers could follow the trails they had blazed.

It is hard to overestimate the part played by the firms of Joseph Simon, the Franks, as well as the Gratz brothers in opening up the lands that were some day to become the states of Ohio, West Virginia, Kentucky, Indiana, Illinois, and Missouri. The first breath of civilization frequently came with these fur traders and hunters who moved in in the regions that they had explored.

Hayman Levy, one of the greatest Jewish merchants of the period, was the head of the New York firm of Levy, Lyons and Company and became the largest fur trader in the colonies. His was one of the principal mercantile firms in the city and had a branch in Europe known as Levy, Solomon and Company. Mr. Levy also carried on an extensive trade for many years among the Indians, by whom he was widely known and with whom he had great influence. He not only purchased all that the Indians brought for traffic, but kept everything in his large establishment to supply their wants. The Indians who came to the city dealt largely with him, and at certain seasons of the year were to be seen in large numbers lining the streets in the vicinity of his warehouse. There are entries in his book that show that he was the first employer of John Jacob Astor, the ancestor of the millionaire Astor of today, who at the time received one dollar a day for beating furs. Nicholas Low, ancestor of President Seth Low of Columbia Col-

lege, served as Levy's clerk for seven years, and then laid
the foundation of his great fortune in hogshead of rum purchased from his former employer, who besides rendered him
substantial assistance.

The restrictive acts of Parliament and the general colonial
policy pursued by the government produced a disasterous
effect upon business and Hayman Levy from his widely extended interests failed in 1768, but his assignees were enabled
to discharge the whole of his indebtedness with interest. The
great fire of 1776 destroyed all his property, yet nothwithstand-
ing all, he carried on his fur trade on his own account until
his death in 1790.

16.   THE FIRST JEWISH CLUB IN AMERICA

As early as 1761, the Jewish merchants of colonial Newport
organized and maintained America's first Jewish social club.
It was much of the same character as those of the English
and Bostonian merchants.

On November 25, 1761 nine men including Moses Lopez,
Isaac Polock, Jacob Isaacs, Abraham Sarzedas, Naphtali Hart,
Moses Levy, Issachar Polock, Naphtali Hart, Jr. and Jacob
Rodriquez Rivera adopted a set of rules for the club which
illustrated both their travelled experience as well as their
urbanity. Inasmuch that it has been recorded that the Newport community in 1760 numbered amongst itself fifty-eight
Jews, the club must have contained a fair proportion of its
adult males. Strangely enough the name of Aaron Lopez, at
this date even though not yet recognized as Newport's greatest
Jewish merchant, but who had already won an important position as merchant and shipowner, does not appear on the list
of members. (See Ch. 17). Accordingly, it has been speculated
that when signatures were obtained, he was away on one of
his frequent business trips.

The club developed at first through more or less informal
meetings with a fine social feature at the end which centered
around an elaborate meal, with formal toasts and liberal allow-

ance of drink. The club met every Wednesday evening during the winter months. After one month or four club nights, a new chairman was elected. Each meeting followed a specific pattern. From five to eight o'clock, each member was at liberty to divert at cards. At eight o'clock an elaborate meal was brought in with formidable potions of wine gathered from famous vineyards of distant lands. Formal toasts then followed. After ten o'clock, at the conclusion of the meal no more games were allowed and club business was attended to.

The members for the most part belonged to St. John's Lodge of Masons, had been founders and supporters of Newport's famous Redwood Library, and were all active in varied aspects of Newport's communal and social life. Their major project was the building of the Touro Synagogue and the majority of them numbered amongst those who had brought Peter Harrison, the famous colonial architect from Boston, who had previously built Kings' Chapel in Boston and Christ Church in Cambridge to build it. To this day the Touro Synagogue remains one of America's and Newport's prized ornaments. (See Ch. 88).

17. THE FIRST JEWISH MERCHANT PRINCE IN AMERICA

In 1658 a group of Jews, most of them refugees of the Spanish Inquisition landed in Newport, Rhode Island to constitute the second Jewish settlement in North America. As time went on other Jews from Holland and the West Indies came to the haven of tolerance set up by Roger Williams. There, Newport Jews, many of them outstanding merchants, were to become the leading business men of their day, both in wealth and in pioneer projects, and were among the first to establish the soapmaking industry in America. They were highly responsible for the high standing which Newport had as a seaport and which it lost after the Revolution.

One of these men, Aaron Lopez, who came to Newport from Lisbon in 1752, became known as the "merchant prince of New England," the first of his race to be so designated. He was one of the first to recognize the commercial possibilities of Newport, with its fine harbor and by 1767 had begun utilizing these advantages to the fullest extent. Through his papers in the Newport Historical Society, we may trace his career from its modest beginnings up to the time when he owned more than thirty vessels, in whole or in part, just before the Revolution. His ships carried American raw products to the Spanish Main, England, and Africa. With his father-in-law, Jacob Rodriquez Rivera, he introduced the sperm oil industry in America and began the manufacture of sperm oil and candles which greatly improved lighting. His business ventures in the whaling industry extened as far as the Falkland Islands. Yet with all the vastness of his enterprise, Lopez was a man of charm and genuine humility. Ezra Stiles, the seventh president of Yale, knew him well and wrote that Lopez "was a merchant of the first eminence; for honor and extent of commerce probably surpassed by no merchant in America . . . Without a single enemy and the most universally beloved by an extensive acquaintance, of any man I ever knew."

Probably no man in the colonies suffered a greater financial loss in the Revolution than did Lopez. From the very start he espoused the patriotic cause and donated much wealth to it, but his jeopardized fleet fell into the hands of the British. When the British occupied Newport, he saw most of his wealth disappear. Every Jew who could get away from the town followed Aaron Lopez to Leicester, Massachusetts, where they constituted the first Jewish settlement in that state. These Jews remained in Leicester during the Revolution, conducting there certain types of business. Lopez erected there a large mansion, which upon his death, according to the terms of his will became the Leicester Academy. This was one of the first gestures of its kind up to this time for large philanthropic gifts were very rare indeed.

18.   THE FIRST PROPOSED UNITED STATES SEAL

In 1776, Benjamin Franklin, Thomas Jefferson, and John Adams recommended for the first official seal of the United States, a design whose theme was the escape of the Israelites from Egypt. It had pictured on it the Israelites crossing the Red Sea, with Pharoah and his legions perishing in the background when they attempted to follow. Rays from a pillar of fire beaming on Moses who is represented as standing on the shore extending his hand over the sea, causing it to overwhelm Pharoh also appeared on the design. Around the edges of this proposed seal ran the motto: "Rebellion to tyrants is obedience to God." This motto pleased Jefferson so much that he took it as his own and had it cut upon his private seal.

It is not surprising that the committee which was appointed the same day that the Declaration of Independence was adopted should propose such a device for a seal as they did. The Founding Fathers of America drew heavily on the Bible and Hebraic tradition in laying the foundation of the new republic. The American Revolution was cradled in the Hebraic love of freedom and liberty. Biblical influence had helped not a little in favoring and strengthening opposition to the parliamentary claim. Several decades before the Declaration of Independence, the Biblical injunction: "Proclaim liberty throughout the land unto all the inhabitants thereof", was inscribed on the Liberty Bell and made the great watchword of the American people.

When the American people were ready to form their own government, they were inspired by the ancient Hebraic commonwealth which was composed of three parts, an elective magistrate, who was called a judge, a council of seventy elders known as the Sanhedrin, and the General Assembly of the people. Following the pattern of this three-fold division they patterned their own government which included an executive or president, a supreme court, and congress.

The piety of Americans of the past is further reflected today in the words of our coinage, "In God We Trust." The Hebraic influences manifest in colonial America were so considerable that the seals of many colleges bore Hebrew inscriptions. To this day the seal of Harvard College is a depiction of the ancient Hebrew breast plate of the Urim and Thumin worn by the priests in the Temple.

19. THE FIRST AMERICAN BORN JEWISH CLERGYMAN

The Reverent Gershom Mendez Sexias who became the minister of the first Jewish congregation in North America, Congregation Shearith Israel in 1766 and who continued in this post for more than fifty years, was the first Jewish clergyman to be born on American soil. Born in New York in 1745, he had received his education as a young boy at the congregational school established at the Shearith Israel (See Ch. 11). His ability to write Hebrew is evidenced by a manuscript copy of a Hebrew address which he wrote for Sampson Simson when the latter was graduated from Columbia College. In the course of his ministry during the few times that he was called upon to cite Jewish law, he was able to refer to the Shulhan Arukh. During the fateful and stirring days of the American Revolution, he was one of the most distinguished non-military figures and earned for himself the title of "Patriot Rabbi." Not merely a patriot but a very firebrand of the Revolution, he was instrumental in persuading his congregation to disband and close its ediface on the approach of the British in 1776. When the British captured New York, he refused to remain and left with the sacred Torah scrolls, ceremonial objects, and prayer books. The greater part of his congregation followed him, first to Stratford, Connecticut, and later to Philadelphia where they remained until after the conflict.

After 1778 Philadelphia was the great refuge of patriots from the thirteen colonies. With the increase of numbers of Philadelphia Jewry, the community in 1782 carried out an old ambition to build a synagogue. For their first minister they engaged the "patriot rabbi" of New York who presided over the dedication of their so-called Mikveh Israel or "Hope of Israel" Congregation and served there during most of the struggle.

The Reverent Gershom Mendez Sexias

After the war the Reverent Sexias returned to New York, and resumed his former pulpit once again and for two generations was repeatedly honored as patriot and citizen.

It was Sexias who was the first minister to abandon the use of Spanish in his sermons for English. He preached the first Thanksgiving sermon ever given by a clergyman in the thirteen colonies and was the first of his denomination to speak in the churches of America. He was also the first clergyman in America to institute a prayer for the government in English. He was the first Jew to hold office as a trustee of Columbia University, a position he retained for twenty-five years. His portrait was struck on a bronze metal issued by Columbia University after his death and a painting of him was hung at Columbia University on its one hundred and seventy-fifth anniversary.

Today as one enters the Synagogue of the Congregation Shearith Israel in New York City, he sees a bronze tablet in which is inscribed in a few words the story of the Reverent Gershom Mendez Sexias, the "patriot rabbi" of the American Revolution.

20.   THE FIRST JEW IN AMERICA TO GIVE HIS LIFE FOR HIS COUNTRY

From 1776 to the present day, men of the Jewish faith have been fighting and dying to help preserve American independence.

Less than a month after the earnest band of patriots in Philadelphia pledged to liberty "our lives, our fortunes, and our sacred honor," Francis Salvador, colorful plantation owner of South Carolina, who won the sobriquet of the "southern Paul Revere," was killed in battle. Salvador, a brilliant young English Jew of Portuguese ancestry, had arrived in Charleston, South Carolina in 1773 to develop extensive family holdings there. He became famous as a soldier, legislature, patriot, and together with Charles Pickney and Edward Rutledge, was among the first revolutionary characters of the state.

In 1774 although a resident of America for only a year, Salvador was elected to the General Assembly of South Carolina, the first Jew in American history and probably the first Jew in the modern world to serve as an elective officer. Because of the active part played by him in the patriotic cause, his district made him their representative to the First and Second Provincial Congresses which actively took steps to revolt against the British. There he was named to various committess concerned with the conduct of the war.

At the very beginning of the revolution, on July 1, 1776, Salvador was killed in an Indian skirmish incited by the English. Together with his friend Williamson, he had set out on an expidition to round up volunteer troups to save the colonists from an Indian attack. In the course of the battle that ensued, Salvador who was only twenty-eight years of age was scalped and killed, unaware of the Declaration of Independence. The whole army regretted his loss, added a Continental Journal, "The Remerance". "..as he was universally loved and esteemed by them."

In the brief period of three years, Salvador, a stranger, and a Jew, sat in the representative assembly of the Provincial Congress, was listened to with unusual respect for one of his youth, and died a patriot of the American Revolution, the first Jew in America to give his life for his country. A memorial plaque dedicated to his memory in 1950 at the time of the Bicentennial celebration of the Jewish community of Charleston reads: "Born an aristocrat, he became a democrat; an Englishman, he cast his lot with America; and true to his ancient faith, he gave his life for new hopes of human liberty and understanding."

21. THE FIRST AMERICAN JEWISH GOVERNMENT BROKER

During the Revolutionary War Jews contributed their full share of patriotism off the battlefield as well as on it. When money was needed in 1776 to support the army of Washington in the field, the names of Jews were conspicuous among the givers. When bills of credit were issued from which the element

of credit was greatly lacking, Jews were conspicuous among
the subscribers.

But the one who did more for the cause of the Revolution
than any other Jewish civilian or soldier, was Haym Salomon
of Philadelphia. He came from Poland in 1772,—the first Polish
Jew of whom we have a record in North America,—and established a business as a commission merchant in New York. Salomon prospered. Although New York was the seat of the British
power in the colonies, he cast his fortunes with the patriotic
Sons of Liberty. At the outbreak of the War, he was imprisoned
by the English and barely escaped hanging for intercepting their
supplies. When it was discovered that he could speak ten languages, he was put to work in a British prison camp as an interpreter. In this capacity he assisted American and French prisoners to escape and finally he himself escaped to Philadelphia.
Had not his health been undermined by imprisonment, he might
have been one of the distinguished band of Jewish patriots
who fought valiently with Washington.

Soon after his arrival in Philadelphia, Salomon opened an
office in a plain little house on Front Street, "between Market
and Arch," as his base of operations and from which he was
to render his magnificent services to the colonies. From the
outset, Haym Salomon succeeded in Philadelphia. Most of the
business of the port was with foreign markets whose trade conditions he knew intimately. His straight-forward, honest methods
of transacting business won him an enviable reputation.

It is significant that Haym Salomon's first official recognition
as an able businessman should have come from an ally of the
young republic and not the republic itself. Soon after his arrival
in American, the French Minister, Chevalier de la Luzerne,
appointed Salomon agent for the French government and pay-
master-general for the French forces in America. In these capa-
cities, he handled huge sums of money, but refused all commission. He considered it his patriotic duty to serve the nation
that had crossed the sea to aid his adopted country. He maintained this policy in all his dealings with the government.

It is apparent from early entries in Robert Morris' diary that
the new Superintendent of Finance negociated with other brok-
ers before he began to write almost daily that memorable

Haym Salomon Monument

phrase, "I sent for Haym Salomon." But he was not long in learning that he needed Salomon's vision, integrity and unselfish devotion to the cause of liberty. From that time on, Salomon was consulted on every operation and his sound judgment and clear thinking saved the colonists immense sums.

Salomon's official title was "Broker to the Office of Finance of the United States": that is he was the broker through whom Robert Morris sold the securities of the weak infant government. Morris received hides, tobacco and agricultural products in lieu of money from the colonies. Salomon sold them for the account of the Federal Treasury. He was also called upon to act as government agent to sell captured enemy merchandise. He sold subsidies to France, Holland and Spain.

Handling hundreds of bills of exchange without commission for the Superintendent of Finance was only part of Haym Salomon's contribution to the cause of Freedom. He also floated loans; he endorsed notes; he contributed generously from his private means to needy soldiers and statesmen; he equipped military units with his own money; he subscribed heavily for all government loans. At his untimely death at the age of forty-five, it is said that he held over a third of a million dollars in paper of the new republic.

This would seem a comfortable legacy for his wife and four children, but unfortunately the sum, badly depreciated, went with other assets to repay what he had contracted in the interest of his country. Haym Salomon died bankrupt, but without dishonor. Although Congress after Congress considered the claims of the Salomon heirs, no compensation or adjustment was ever made.

As an ardent Jew, Salomon was one of the founding members and a trustee of the Congregation Mikve Israel, Philadelphia's first synagogue. In 1783 he was one of the five Philadelphian Jews who in behalf of the Philadelphia Jewish Community, petitioned to the Council of Censors of Pennsylvania for the removal of the obnoxious requirement of the Test Oath of the state which demanded that each member elected to the assembly should affirm that both "the Scriptures of the Old and New Testament were given by divine inspiration."

A loyal and unselfish patriot of his adopted country, the

debt of gratitude that the nation owes Salomon was in part paid by the erection of a statue in Chicago showing George Washington with his arms about Robert Morris and Haym Salomon. Some years ago, Warner Brothers made a short moving picture called "My Country First" written by George Jessel, the celebrated actor, which concerned some of the highlights of the life of Haym Salomon.

22. THE FIRST COOPERATIVE CHARITY VENTURE

Mordecai Sheftall, who was the first white child and the first Jew to be born in Savannah, Georgia and in the South, was the original Jewish founding member of the Union Society, the first cooperative charity venture in America which sought to unite in its work, Protestants, Catholics and Jews in the belief that men of different faiths could work together for a common social cause. The society exerted a profound influence for social betterment during the early history of Georgia.

When the Revolution broke out, Sheftall threw himself completely into the work and was made chairman of the Parochial Committee which was organized by the patriots to help take care of the affairs of Georgia and united all the different religious denominations in its work. This position earned for him the title of "very great rebel."

As the war progressed he was appointed Commissary-General to the troops of Georgia as well as to the Continental troops. When the British attacked and took possession of Savannah, Sheftall, who took part in the defence of the city was imprisoned. In 1779 he was paroled after promising not to take an active part in the war and was exchanged for a prisoner of equal rank.

While prisoners of war, Sheftall and two other fellows continued to hold meetings of the Union Society to keep it alive. In 1825, when Lafayette laid the cornerstone of the Pulaski monument in Savannah, a relic was deposited within it with the words: "a piece of oaktree from Sunbury County, Georgia, under which in 1779 the charter of the Union Society was pre-

served and Mr. Mordecai Sheftall, then a prisoner of war was
elected president."

Moses Sheftall, the son of Mordecai Sheftall, who was born
in Savannah in 1769 was the first Jewish doctor born in America. In 1804 he established the first medical society in Georgia
and did much to raise the standards of the medical profession.
During the War of 1812 he volunteered for service in the army.
Upon his return he was the first Jew in Georgia to be elected
judge of the county court and was not long afterwards elected
to the state legislature.

23.   THE FIRST JEWISH LAWYER IN AMERICA

In New Amsterdam, as New York was called during the Dutch
regime, there was no such thing as a class of professional lawyers. Cases were tried before the court, but neither magistrate
nor those who pleaded them had any legal education. For
example, the name of Solomon Pietersen, the earliest one that
we have on record, appears as attorney in 1654, in the court
records of New Amsterdam, although he had no legal training.
No name is more prominent than that of Asser Levy whose
almost uniform success against Governor Stuyvesant in defend-
ing the rights of his people accounts for the fact that he appears
as attorney for others also.

The colonial colleges for the most part catered primarily to
the prospective clergymen and at a later date to attorneys. At
that time Jews were businessmen and merchants, not ministers
or lawyers. Merchants' sons who might follow in their father's
footsteps did not receive an academic education in those days.

Philadelphia, was the seat of culture, one of the great educational centers in the new world. Not a few of the institutions
of the city bore the imprint of Benjamin Franklin, who was the
founder of the College of Philadelphia, later to be known as
the University of Pennsylvania. The prepartory school associated with the College was called the Academy. Five Jewish
boys were enrolled there before 1770. One of these lads, Moses
Levy who was born in Philadelphia, the son of a prominent

merchant and a signer of the Non-Importation Resolution, completed the college course and received an A.B. degree in the class of 1772. He was the only Jewish graduate of the institution in pre-Revolutionary times. After continuing his course of studies in the Law School, he was admitted to the Bar in 1778 to become America's first Jewish lawyer. In a short time, he became one of the foremost lawyers of his time. After serving his state in the Legislature he became presiding judge of the District Court of Philadelphia, a position he retained until 1825. For a quarter of a century before his death he was a trustee of the University of Pennsylvania. He also appears to have been a man of property for he sold his house on Chestnut Street for $10,000 to the Bank of North America, the first Bank in the United States.

As council in many cases and because of his brilliant record as judge, Levy won the highest esteem of his associates on the Philadelphia bench and bar. At one time his name was even mentioned in the Jefferson-Gallatin correspondence as a worthy candidate for the Office of Attorney-General of the United States.

President Jefferson wanted to appoint Moses Levy in his Cabinet for the post and on September 1, 1804, wrote to Gallatin, the Secretary of the Treasury the following: "I ask the favor of you to inquire fully into the legal knowledge, judgment, and moral and social character of Levy. We must have none, but a good-humored man." Gallatin replied, "As a lawyer he is superior to Dickerson, and would, I presume, do tolerably well."

24. THE FIRST JEWISH MAJOR IN AMERICA

Benjamin Nones, one of a group of Frenchman who had come to America in 1777, at about the time that Lafayette arrived, is America's first Jewish major. Believing heart and soul in freedom, he left his thriving wine business behind in Bordeaux and came to the assistance of the embattled Americans.

Soon after his arrival in Philadelphia, he enlisted as a volunteer in the Continental Army and at first served as a private under the command of Pulaski and then under De Kalb. When De Kalb fell in the Battle of Camden in 1780, Nones together with three other officers, members of his own faith, removed him from the battlefield. Nones was promoted to staff officer and finally major under Washington and Lafayette. In this capacity, he led a unit into battle that was almost entirely composed fo Jews. In recognition of his services, he was awarded a special certificate and earned for himself the title of the "Jewish Lafayette."

Nones was as much devoted to his religion as he was to his country. Soon after his joining the army, he spoke to his superior officer explaining that he was a Jew and respectfully asked to be exempt from military duties on the Sabbath. The officer was very much impressed by the boy's attachment to his faith and ordered that the boy be permitted to observe the Sabbath. This order which was the first of its kind ever to be issued in America, is still preserved to this very day in the annals of the Revolutionary War.

When the War ended, Nones returned to Philadelphia, married and raised a large family. He was elected president of Philadelphia's first synagogue, a position he retained for many years. In addition he ran for public office. We have preserved a most interesting campaign letter in which he tells that he is accused of being a Jew, of being a Republican, and of being poor. He proudly states that he is all three of these terrible things, which in his opinion make him even more worthy of election.

25. THE FIRST JEWISH INSURER IN AMERICA

For many years the ships that sailed out of America with cargoes for Europe and Asia were insured, if they were insured at all, in London. The only way that the owner of a ship could insure it against the risks of shipwreck, piracy, and other ocean dangers was to take out a policy of Lloyd's of London. But by the eighteenth century sea traffic was so heavy that it seemed sensible to transfer the writing of insurance to Boston. Moses Michael Hays was the first Jew to open a marine insurance office in Boston. Setting himself up at 68 State Street, for the owner of a ship about to sail, Hays would make out a policy, describing the vessel, the voyage it was to make, the rate and amount of insurance. Bostonian merchants who wished to share in the risk signed their names to the policy with the amounts they were willing to underwrite. He did very well in business and at a later date added to this "an Assurance Office for houses and household goods from loss and damage from fire, in any part of the Province." In 1784 a group of nine merchants called upon him to help make plans for a bank which would serve them as the bank of England then did, by receiving deposits and discounting loans. This bank became the direct decendent of the First National Bank of Boston, the largest in New England and one of the ten largest in the United States.

Hays was respected in the community not only for his wealth, but for his many personal virtues and sound advice. He was the son of a New York merchant and had started life there as a watchmaker in 1769 when he had been admitted a freeman. He was a brother-in-law of Rabbi Isaac Touro of the Newport Syngogue and in 1770 had moved to Newport, where he set up a modest shop as a general merchant "on the point near Holmes Wharf". He went through years of hard sledding and finally moved to Boston where he attained wealth and a position of prominence. He became a leading figure in Masonic circles as well and was responsible for the introduction into the country of the "Ancient Accepted Scottish Rite" of masonry which comprised thirty-three degrees. In recognition of the powers conferred upon him, he was elected Grand Master of the Grand Lodge at annual elections from 1788 to 1792. In 1793 he became a member of a subordinate lodge and was again elected Grand Master. Paul Revere served as a deputy grandmaster under him. His son and grandsons constituted the only masons in Massachusetts before 1810.

Hays was the first Jewish benefactor of Harvard College and appears on the donors list as early as 1780.

He died in Boston in 1805 and was buried in the Jewish ceme-

tery in Newport. In his obituary, the "Boston Centinel" wrote:
"He walked abroad fearing no man, but loving all . . . . . .
He was without guile, detesting hypocracy as he despised
meanness! Take him for all in all, he was indeed a man."

26. THE FIRST JEW
TO FOUND A SETTLEMENT IN THE UNITED STATES

The first town in America planned by and named for a Jew
is Aaronsburg, Pennsylvania, which soon after its founding acquired a population of two hundred and fifty.

It all happened on October 5, 1786, when the state conveyed
land to Aaron Levy, an Indian trader and land speculator
whose dealings ranged through the frontier of the colony and
the state of Pennsylvania. Levy, who was well-known in the
community, had come to America from Holland in 1760 while
still in his teens and became one of the patriots of the American Revolution. With other patriots he had risked losing his
life at the hands of the British by giving aid to the rebels. He
was at times associated with the Gratz brothers of Philadelphia,
with Robert Morris and James Wilson. Most of his life he lived
on the frontier himself, in Northumberland County, where his
tract of land was located. As he grew older, he apparently
needed Jewish communal life, and ultimately moved back to
the more settled areas, first to Lancaster and then to Philadelphia.

In June 1779, Mr. Levy had bought of a Mr. Wetzel a large
tract of land and several years later, when finally acquired of
him, planned the town of Aaronsburg. The town in all comprised six hundred and twelve lots, each measuring sixty by
two hundred and thirty feet. Upon this tract houses were laid
out with much taste and good skill. In the naming of streets,
Levy used personal names and named one of them in honor
of his wife Rachael. In his vast real-estate dealings he was represented by Judge Moses Levy of the Philadelphia Bar. (See
Ch. 23).

On the occasion of the one hundred and fiftieth anniversary

of the founding of the town, it was the scene of a great demonstration when thirty thousand Americans of all faiths spent a
Sunday there to celebrate. The event received national publi-
city. Public figures including Justice Felix Frankfurter of the
United States Supreme Court, Dr. Ralph Bunche, United Nations Nobel Prize winner, and the Rev. Daniel Poling, prominent clergyman, spoke on interfaith good-will as the American
way of life.

Today, there is an unbroken line of villages and towns from
Aaronsburg, Pennsylvania, that extends across the country
along the old trails to Roseville, California, and Heppner, Oregon, named after hardy Jewish souls, who like Aaron Levy
brought with them the first breath of civilization to hitherto
untrampled territory.

27. THE FIRST JEWISH BOOKDEALER IN AMERICA

As the years went by schools grew in numbers and people
became more interested in books and learning. In the year
1791 the first American Jewish bookdealer opened his shop. Benjamin Gomez, the owner, was a man of intelligence and high
character. He stemmed from a distinguished family of Spanish
Marranos who had originated in Madrid and who has established themselves in the United States at the beginning of the
eighteenth century. His father was Louis Gomez, one of New
York's principal merchants and who had proved a very material addition to the little New York community in which he was
the recognized head for many years.

Benjamin Gomez first appeared in the New York directory
of 1791 as a bookseller, when he was located at 32 Maiden
Lane "near the Fly Market" where his brother, Isaac Gomez,
carried on business as a broker. Gomez was one of the biggest
booksellers of the day and also sold stationery. A few months
after he opened his shop, Gomez ran a full page notice in a
local paper to say that he had many volumes for sale including
some that were "just imported from Dublin." Although there
were no detective stories or novels in his book shop, he offered

a very wide choice of books. All the books were on religious, historical, or scientific subjects and ranged from the Bible, Shakespeare, and "Arabian Nights" to books on anatomy. The following year he extended his bookselling to include publishing. Twenty-one of the books which he published are still known to us. They include Hugh Gaines' edition of "Pilgrims Progress," (1794), an abridged edition of "Robinson Crusoe" (1795), "Captain Cook's Third and Last Voyage", (1795), as well as "The Sorrows of Werther" (1795).

After a few years Gomez moved to new quarters at 97 Maiden Lane and his success was sufficient to cause Naphtalie Judah of New York in 1795 to enter the trade as America's second Jewish bookseller.

28.   THE FIRST AMERICAN PRESIDENTIAL RESIDENCE OWNED BY A JEW   ......

The American Jew can point with pride to the part played by our people in colonial and revolutionary times. In private life George Washington had met Jews at an early date. For example, Hezekiah Levy was a member of the Fredericksburg Lodge in Virginia, in 1771, Washington's own Masonic Lodge. Later, during the ensuing struggle for independence, he came to know several Jewish soldiers. One of the most prominent of them was Colonel Isaac Franks, who at the age of seventeen, shortly after the Battle of Lexington, when the Revolution first broke out into open warfare, enlisted in the rebel army. He fought under the immediate command of Washington in the Battle of Long Island and earned for himself the title of "Washington's right-hand-man." He was wounded several times, taken prisoner by the British, but managed to escape. In due time he received various promotions in the infantry and quartermasters department of the Pennsylvania militia.

With the war over, Franks now a lieutenant-colonel, he returned to public life. He became one of Washington's closest friends who never forgot him. It was in speaking of Franks that the president said: "He was a soldier who served his country well and was concerned more with the welfare of his country than the glory of his person."

The years immediately following the war find him in reduced circumstances, but later his fortunes improved. He acquired a home in Germantown which was known to be comfortable. During the winter of 1793, when a yellow fever epedemic was raging in Philadelphia, President Washington occupied this house as his presidential residence at which time the seat of government was temporarily removed from Philadelphia to Germantown.

The bill of occupancy which was presented to the president is highly amusing. In addition to the rent which was sixty-six dollars for two months, Washington paid for a missing flatiron, four platters, and one fork. He was also charged for "the damage done to a large Japand waiter made use of in the service of the president." The sum of two dollars and fifty cents was expended by Franks "for cleaning my house and putting it in the same condition the President rec'd it in."

For many years Franks continued to be a prosperous citizen. During the last four years of his life he was the recipient of a Revolutionary pension and held several civil posts. He was the first Jew to sit for Gilbert Stuart, who is famous for his portarits of Washington and other colonial leaders.

29. THE FIRST COPPER ROLLING MILL IN AMERICA

The first copper rolling mill in America was built by Harmon Hendricks at Soho, New Jersey in 1812. The mill is still operated and owned by the descendants of Harmon Hendricks. The firm of Hendricks Brothers is the oldest Jewish business concern in the United States with a continuous history and is the second oldest firm in America.

As early as 1764, Uriah Hendricks, the father of Harmon, established a business in metals in New York, soon after his arrival from Holland. In 1776 his name appears as one of the signers of the loyalist address to General Howe. His grand-son Uriah Hendricks II, carried on the work of the firm and in turn handed it down to his four sons.

Harmon Hendricks was active in Jewish communal affairs as well and in 1824 was chosen president of the Shearith Israel Congregation in New York. During the War of 1812, he gave $40,000 as a government loan when the government was having difficulty with the sale of war bonds. This was one of the largest individual subscriptions for bonds ever made in the entire annals of American history up to that date.

Uriah Hendricks is buried in New York's oldest Jewish cemetery which dates back to 1656. (See Ch. 8).

30.   THE FIRST AMERICAN JEWISH HEROINE OF FICTION

Rebecca Gratz, the rich, beautiful, idealistic belle of Philadelphia society, the daughter of the great Philadelphian merchant, Michael Gratz, is the first American Jewess upon whom literary immortality has been conferred. She is the original of the character "Rebecca" in Sir Walter Scott's novel "Ivanhoe."

Her purity of heart, beauty of face and loyalty to her race inspired the imagination of her friend, Washington Irving, who knew her well. Washington Irving's beloved Matilda Hoffman died of consumption in 1809 and had been nursed tenderly for the last six months of her life by Rebecca, who had been her childhood friend. Going abroad to bury his grief Irving visited and became friendly with Sir Walter Scott, then at the height of his fame and all but the acknowleged author of the Waverly Novels. He told the great author about her, and when he wrote "Ivanhoe" he drew the character of his Rebecca from the description of Rebecca Gratz given by his American friend. Two years later Scott sent his story to Irving with a note expressing the hope that the "Rebecca" of "Ivanhoe" typified all that was noble in the real "Rebecca." The qualities described in "Ivanhoe" precisely fitted the original Rebecca, and are the ones for which Scott's "Rebecca" has become such a popular heroine.

(*Courtesy of the American Jewish Historical Society*)
A painting of Rebecca Gratz by Thomas Sully

Outgrowing the romantic legend of her life, Rebecca Gratz became a leading worker for charity and education in Philadelphia and devoted her life in doing good to others. In 1801 she became the tireless secretary of the first society organized to help the poor of Philadelphia, a non-sectarian organization known as the "Female Association for the Relief of Women and Children in Reduced Circumstances." In 1819 she organized the first "Jewish Women's Aid Society" to care for the large number of Jewish immigrants who were then entering the United States. When there were orphans to take care of, Rebecca started the first Jewish orphan asylum in her city and the first in America, and was its secretary for forty years. After having observed how the Christians taught their children religion one day a week, she drew up the plans for the first Jewish Sunday School in America and was its president and supervisor for twenty-five years. (See Ch. 11).

When she died at the age of eighty-eight, she was mourned as the foremost lady in the United States and one of the noblest women in the world.

31.   THE FIRST JEWISH NEWSPAPERS IN AMERICA

The first Jewish newspaper published in America devoted exclusively to Jewish affairs was known as "The Jew." It was published monthly in New York beginning in March 1823 by Solomon Henry Jackson, the first Jewish printer in the city of New York, who had a virtual monopoly of all synagogue printing.

"The Jew" which ran for two years was published primarily as a defense of Judaism against all adversaries and particularly against the insidious attacks of the "Israel Advocate" which as house organ of the "American Society for the Amelioration of the Condition of the Jew," a missionary society, had set about spreading false ideas about the Jew. It sold for a dollar fifty a year and was delivered to New York subscribers at their dwellings and to distant subscribers through the New York Post Office.

In 1825, when Jackson's paper was discontinued, the Jews of New York had to rely on the local press for news of Jewish interest until 1843, when the Reverent Isaac Leeser, outspoken educator and opponent of slavery had founded "The Occident," in Philadelphia. By 1849, however, New York Jews began to venture into the field of Jewish periodical publication and thereafter the community never lacked organs for the dissemination of news among its members. In that year there appeared in German "Israel's Herold" which was launched by Isidor Bush, a recently arrived refugee from the Austrian counter-revolution of 1848. The purpose of "Israel's Herold" was to bring about unity among the Jews," regardless of religious, social, and political differences.

In the fifties, "The Asmonean," described as a "Family Journal of Commerce, Politics, Religion and Literature," published by Robert Lyon, an English Jew, built up a fairly large following, and became the first successful Jewish weekly in America. Its pages reflect the life, manners, folkways, opinions and anecdotes of the day and it was at its peak in 1855. With the rise of other periodicals it began to decline. Dr. Isaac M. Wise, the founder of Reform Judaism in America, began publishing "The Israelite" in Cincinnati. In San Francisco there was the paper called "The Weekly Gleaner", while in Chicago there was "The Chicago Israelite." In Baltimore, Dr. David Einhorn edited "Sinai," a monthly which ran for six years. In 1857 "The Jewish Messenger" was founded in New York and appeared weekly. In 1902 it united with "The American Hebrew," a conservative organ, and is still being published today under that name.

As the earlier periodicals left the field, they beckoned onward and called for successors. Various weekly magazines and newspapers were projected from time to time and ranged from humorous, illustrated journals, periodic story-books, miscellanies of holiday literature, to the splendid literary and scientific monthly "Commentary." In 1948, the "American Jewish Daily" appeared. These periodicals added color, picturesqueness, and cultural content to the domain of Jewish newspaperdom.

Some attempts were made to publish Yiddish newspapers in the New World even before the stream of Jewish immigration began to flow from Eastern Europe in 1880. In 1870, J. K.

Buchner founded the "Yiddishe Zeitung" in New York, and two years later, Kasriel H. Sarasohn established the "New Yorker Yiddishe Zeitung." They were both weeklies and both suspended publication after a struggle of several months. The "Israelitische Presse," founded in Chicago in 1879, was also short-lived. "Der New Yorker Israelit" was a similar, unsuccessful venture of Mordecai Yohalimstein in 1875. Sarasohn, however, who was to become the successful pioneer in the field, began to publish the "Yiddishe Gazette" in 1874. This had a better reception than his previous undertaking, for by this time the Jewish population had been augmented by a considerable influx of new arrivals. By 1885 Sarasohn felt sufficiently encouraged to launch a Yiddish daily. Thus the "Yiddish Tageblatt" was born. It continued for many years to be the outstanding exponent of Orthodox Judaism and the foremost supporter of the Zionist ideal. In 1928 it united with the "Jewish Morning Journal" and is still being published today under that name.

The second daily to be established was "Der Taegliche Herold," founded in 1891; the third daily was the "Abendblatt," organ of the Jewish labor elements and socialist groups, established in 1894. Out of a division in the ranks of the radicals came a new paper, the "Forward," founded by Abraham Cahan, which supplanted the "Abendblatt." The "Forward," today, with its positive position on all Jewish questions and its enthusiastic support of Zionism and Israel has the largest circulation of any foreign language newspaper in this country.

Jacob Saphirstein, Louis E. Miller, Herman Bernstein, Jacob Fishman, and Rev. Harris Masliansky were among the other notable personalities associated with the launching of memorable Yiddish dailies, the chain of such papers having been extended to a number of cities like Boston, Chicago, Philadelphia and Cleveland as well as many others.

32. THE FIRST AMERICAN ZIONIST

Mordecai Manuel Noah who in 1824 had declared, "We will return to Zion as we went forth, bringing the faith we carried away with us," is considered the first American Zionist. With this statement, he had anticipated almost by a century, the Zionism of today.

Noah's career was a varied one. He was born in Philadelphia in 1785, the son of a soldier of the Revolutionary War. The elder Noah, it was believed by some, had won the friendship of his commander, George Washington, who actually attended his wedding. During his lifetime, Manuel Noah worked at many things. He was a newspaperman. He edited among other papers, "The New York Enquirer," "Evening Star," and "The Union." He helped James Gordon Bennett to found "The New York World." He wrote plays and studied law. He also served as a judge, sheriff, and Surveyor of the Port of New York. But his great enthusiasm was for the history of the Jewish people.

In 1813 President Madison appointed him as American consul to Tunis, thus making him the first Jew in America to hold a high diplomatic post in the foreign service of his country. Noah felt very sorry over the plight of the homeless Jews in the Orient and in Europe, and it was here that he began to think and dream of a land for them. He wanted to see Palestine returned to them, but knowing how difficult it would be to obtain such a concession from the Orient rulers, his thoughts turned to the great open spaces of America. It was after his return from Algiers, that he sought to found an island of asylum in Grand Island, opposite Buffalo, New York for the oppressed Jews of the world. He wrote an appeal to the Jews throughout the world calling upon them to come and settle in the new colony which he named "Ararat," which was to be under the protection of the United States.

This, the grand scheme of his life, however, proved a failure. There was no rush to accept the offer of refuge; not a single building was erected on the island; even the monument raised to commemorate the venture was finally lost.

But Noah did not despair when the island of his dreams remained a wilderness. Twenty years later we find him writing

a pamphlet urging the rebuilding of Palestine. Little did he realize that fifty years later, another dreamer and man of action, Theodor Herzl would call upon the Jews of the world to follow him to Palestine and that he would receive an answer. (see Ch. 59).

33. THE FIRST REFORM CONGREGATION IN AMERICA

Strictly orthodox in their religion, the Spanish and Portuguese Jews established six Jewish congregations and planted the seeds of Judaism in American soil. The early German immigration brought new blood into the Jewish communities and also brought the seeds of the Reform movement which had begun in Germany in the early years of the century.

At that time the old Sephardic congregation of Charleston, South Carolina, Congregation Kahal Kodesh Beth Elohim, was the largest and richest in the United States. Although it had been founded by the Sephardim and followed their ritual as well as the custom of complete religious domination over the members of the congregation, it included a large portion of German Jews.

In 1824, a group of forty-seven members petitioned the trustees for reforms in the services and ritual to effect "a more wholesome, and more respectable state of discipline." First they asked that:

With regard to such parts of the service as it is desired should undergo this change, your memorialists would strenuously recommend that the most solemn portions be retained and everything superfluous excluded; and that the principal parts, and if possible all that is read in HEBREW, should also be read in ENGLISH, so as to enable every member of the congregation fully to understand every part of the service.

Secondly, they asked that Sabbath services should be abridged; thirdly, that the custom of offerings at the alter, then still recited in the Spanish language be abolished and the synagogue rely wholly on membership subscriptions; and finally that there be an English sermon weekly.

When the trustees rejected the petition and changes in the services were refused, a new group was organized under the name of "Reform Society of Israelites," under the leadership of Isaac Harby, a Charleston born schoolmaster and well-known journalist of his day. This society lasted for eight years. The congregation had no rabbi and its services were conducted and the sermons preached by laymen. Abraham Moise, David Nunes Carvalho and Isaac Harby prepared and printed a prayer book in which there appeared many Christian hymns. They voiced their own Articles of Faith without presuming "to restrict the faith or conscience of any man."

By its first anniversary the congregation had fifty members. In 1833 at a meeting, the society decided to abandon its fight for reform and passed out of existence.

By 1840, twenty-two of the original seceders rejoined Beth Elohim where Rabbi Gustavus Poznanski was the new preacher and chazzan. He was a Polish Jew who had lived some years in Hamburg and had known the Hamburg Temple, the cradle of Reform Judaism. In 1840, the cornerstone of a new synagogue was laid to replace the old synagogue which had been destroyed in the fire of 1838. Before the new building was completed, thirty-eight members petitioned the trustees "that an organ be erected in the Synagogue to assist in the vocal parts of the services."

In his dedication sermon, not only did Rabbi Poznanski approve of the use of the organ, but declared the observance of the second day of the festivals to be unnecessary and recommended its abandonment. Thus Reform Judaism took root in the United States.

Under the leadership of Rabbi Isaac M. Wise who had come to America from Bohemia in 1846, the practices and philosophy of Judaism were subject to further modernization. Other changes in Jewish ceremony and the introduction of English in the religious services were accompanied by strife and dissensions between its Orthodox and Reform members.

The Union of American Hebrew Congregations, the Hebrew

Union College and the Central Conference of American Rabbis, were all the offspring of the work of Rabbi Isaac M. Wise.

To the Orthodox Jews, Reform Judaism was not only distateful but shocking. Convinced that Reform would spell the downfall of Judaism, the Orthodox leaders, all of them East European Jews, carried on a bitter and relentless fight against Reform. The Russian Jews brought with them from the Old Country the religious cult known as Chassidism and established it in America. They built hundreds of synagogues, established Talmud Torahs, founded the Jewish Theological Seminary and Yeshiva College. They made America into the center of Judaism and preserved Orthodoxy. It is really doubtful whether without them Judaism would have survived the influence of assimilation and reform.

34. THE FIRST JEWISH POETESS IN AMERICA

Jews have made many and varied contributions to American literature. The earliest Jewish poetess of whom we have a record is Penina Moise of Charleston, South Carolina. An extremely pious Jewess, nurtured on the best in French and English literature, she excelled in devotional poetry written in classical manner and meter.

Miss Moise was born in Charleston in 1797, the daughter of Sarah and Abraham Moise. Her father died when she was twelve years old and she was left to support her paralyzed mother and large family. She had to work hard to battle against poverty but still managed to study and write. As a child she was nearsighted and to overcome her own feeling of inferiority would find escape in reading, often giving it her every spare moment. At an early age her literary ability began to make itself manifest and by 1833 her poems began to appear in print regularly.

In 1835 a small book of her poems "Fancy's Sketch Book" was published. She became known the country over and people looked forward to her poems which appeared as often as three

times a week in "The Charleston Courier." She was also a con-
tributor to "The Charleston Book" in 1845 along with the best
names among the writers of Charleston. She wrote for "Godey's
Lady's Book," "The Boston Daily Times," "The New Orleans
Commercial Times," and "The Washington Union." Her poetry
on Jewish themes appeared in such periodicals as Isaac Leeser's
publication "The Occident." "The Rejection of the Jew Bill in
the House of Lords" (1833), "The Jew of Damasucus," (1840),
and "To Sir Moses Montifiore" were among her most popular
poems.

Her best work is a volume of Hebrew Hymns which appeared
in 1856. She wrote the hymns for the use of Congregation Beth
Elohim when the Reform service was introduced. The collection was reprinted a number of times and now there are more
of her hymns in the hymnal of the Union of American Hebrew
Congregations (the Reform group), than that of any other
writer.

Penina Moise was also a teacher. She taught at Kahal Kodesh
Beth Elohim's Sabbath School which was organized only a
few months after Rebecca Gratz established the first Sunday
School in Philadelphia. She also conducted an exceptionally fine
girls' school for many years, although she became totally blind
in her later life.

She died in 1880 at the age of eighty-three. Her last words
were:

"Lay no flowers on my grave. They are for those who live in
the sun, and I have always lived in the shadow."

In 1911 the Charleston section of the Council of Jewish
Women piously published a selection of Penina Moise's poetry
and some of her prose.

35.   THE FIRST JEWISH WOMAN REFORMER IN AMERICA

At the time that women in America were rebelling at their
lack of independence in a changing world, Ernestine L. Rose,
a rabbi's daughter, circulated the first petition for the property
rights of women. As early as 1837 she appeared before the

New York State legislature to fight for the passage of the liberalizing statute, a fight she continued for over nine years.

A practical idealist, constructive, and keen minded, her development and career had been extraordinary. She was born in Russian Poland in 1810 and died in London in 1892. As a child she studied the Scriptures and was observant in her practice of Judaism, but at fourteen she accumulated a great many doubts. At seventeen she left home to become an apostle of humanitarianism. She traveled far and wide at her own expense, and held forth on a broad range of reform topics. Speaking with a slight and attractive foreign accent, using animated, fluent, direct and impressive language, she advocated free public schools and called attention to the existing evils of the social system, wickedness of slavery, injustices to women, and the shortcomings of human character. Wherever she went, she lifted the hearts of her listeners and bound them together in the magical bond of understanding. Many of her speeches showed the influence of Robert Owen, the English Utopian Socialist whom she met in 1832, four years prior to her coming to America.

In 1850, she was elected delegate to the first National Woman's Rights Convention in Worcester, Massachusetts. Here she met such liberal leaders as Lucrecia Mott, Lucy Stone, William Lloyd Garrison and Wendell Philips, all advocates of woman's rights, abolitionism and religious liberty. She continued as delegate to all the Woman's Rights Conventions every year thereafter until the time of her death.

During the Civil War she joined with Elizabeth Stanton and Susan B. Anthony, Mrs. Chalkstone, a Jewess and other anti-slavery crusaders to form the Woman's National Loyal League and was active in collecting signatures to petition President Lincoln to issue the Emancipation Proclamation.

She was the first to begin woman suffrage agitation in the West, and was largely responsible for the adoption of woman suffrage by the state of Wyoming in 1869. However, she did not live long enough to see the fruits of her labor which was finally enacted into the Nineteenth Amendment in 1920.

36. THE FIRST PUBLICATIONS
ON AMERICAN JEWISH HISTORY

The first attempt in America of writing Jewish history was undertaken by Cotton Mather, the personification of Puritanism and its most learned minister. Unpublished, in six large volumes, in the Archives of the Massachusetts Historical Society in Boston, his "Biblia Americana" may still be seen today. Mather had always shown a keen interest in Jews and in Hebrew and in 1693, when only thirty-one years of age, began a history of the Jews from Biblical times up to his own day. However, his labor was not finished and although he worked on what he calls "one of the greatest works that I ever undertook in my life" for seven years, it never got into print.

Lee Friedman, the eminent Jewish historian and president of the American Jewish Historical Society, tells us that a long interval ensued before Robert Thomas' curious medley was published in 1791 at Boston, under the title of "A Brief Account of the Persecutions of the Jews," in the first "Old Farmers' Almanic." Although the very first narration of post-biblical Jewish history to get into print, it was merely journalistic.

The second serious attempt by an American to write a post-biblical history of the Jews was not made until 1812. In that year the Boston blue-stocking Hannah Adams, published "The History of the Jews from the Destruction of Jerusalem to the Nineteenth Century." Hannah Adams had shown an active interest in the conversion of the Jews and was associated with America's first missionary society for the conversion of the Jews—"The American Society for Meliorating the Condition of the Jews." Although the book went through several editions, only a single chapter of eighteen pages is devoted to the "Jews in America."

It was not until thirty years later, in 1842, that Jewish history written by a Jewish author came to be published. In that year, Joseph Jonas, the first Jewish pioneer of the Ohio Valley who had settled there as early as 1817, submitted a series of articles to "The Occident," the first successful Jewish periodical, entitled "The Jews of the Ohio Valley." The problems of the isolated Jew, the struggle to build up a religious community, the

tendency to modify ritual and custom, the debate as to the forms
of Jewish education, and the relation to the non-Jews are all
reflected here. Subsequently this proved to be a valuable source
of information concerning the history of the early pioneers.

In 1854, Rabbi Isaac M. Wise in Albany printed a first volume
of a "History of the Israelitish Nation From Abraham to the
Present Time"; but he apparently abandoned the plan and left
the work unfinished before he reached post-biblical times.

The first complete history of the Jews in America did not
appear until 1888 when Isaac Markens published "The Hebrews
in America." This was followed in 1893 by the more popularly
known "Settlement of the Jews in America" by Charles P. Daly.
The same year in answer to a call issued by Dr. Cyrus Adler
of the Jewish Theological Seminary, the American Jewish Historical Society was founded. It began collecting early records,
minute books of congregations, as well as fraternal lodge letters,
manuscripts and documents affecting early American Jewish
history. The publications of this society have brought to light
a vast amount of information in the reconstruction of American
Jewish history, especially concerning the early Jewish settlements
in the East.

In 1947 one of the phases of the newly expanded program of
the Hebrew Union-Jewish Institute of Religion has been the
establishment of the American Jewish Archives under the direction of Dr. Jacob R. Marcus. Dedicated to the preservation
of American Jewish historical records and their study, the American Jewish Archives does not compete with, but rather supple-
ments, the American Jewish Historical Society which is located
in New York City and headed by Rabbi Isadore Meyer, its editor
and librarian.

The creation of the American Jewish Archives in Cleveland,
the oldest Jewish settlement west of the Alleghenies, is but
one phase in the inevitable geographical expansion of American
Jewish culture. We may assume that it is but a matter of time
before a similar archive will be established on the Pacific Coast.
This Jewish academic expansion is a repetition of the story of
the development of the general non-Jewish American historical
societies throughout the nation.

37. THE FIRST NATIONAL
JEWISH ORGANIZATION IN AMERICA

The first national Jewish organization to be formed in the United States and still the most important in its influence and work is the Independent Order B'nai B'rith or Sons of the Covenant. It was started in 1843 in New York by twelve German Jews who called themselves "Bundes Bruder" for the purpose of ameliorating the regrettable conditions of hatred and disunity then existing among America's Jews. The founders were all humble men; shopkeepers and artisans of whom the acknowledged leader was Henry Jones.

Unlike some other organizations which began as local clubs and then spread, by chance to national proportions, B'nai B'rith was planned from the beginning as a national body with the noblest purposes. The Preamble to the B'nai B'rith Constitution is still the Preamble today:

"B'nai B'rith has taken upon itself the mission of uniting Israelites in the work of promoting their highest interests and those of humanity; of developing and elevating the mental and moral character of the people of our faith; of incalculating the purest principles of philanthropy, honor and patriotism; of supporting science and art; alleviating the wants of the poor and needy; visiting and attending the sick; coming to the rescue of victims of persecution; providing for, protecting and assisting the widow and orphan on the broadest principles of humanity."

At first the order grew slowly in different parts of the country. By 1858 it had acquired 3,000 members. Although in theory any Jew was eligible for membership, in practice the first members were all German Jews and for the first seven years all club proceedings were conducted in that language. It was only later that the Order succeeded — an absolutely unique achievement in bringing together in the same lodge the rich and the poor, the German and the Russian, the Pole and the Rumanian, the Orthodox and the Reform.

During the post-Civil War days it had acquired 20,000 members and has been growing steadily ever since, being divided into several Grand Lodges throughout the country. Along with philanthropic work such as the erection of orphan homes and old people's homes for the needy, B'nai B'rith began to take steps to protect and aid the Jews everywhere. Out of this grew the Anti-Defamation League to protect the good name of the Jew in America.

The B'nai B'rith spread to foreign lands in 1882 and in time lodges have been organized in England, Turkey, as well as in Israel, with the Constitutional Grand Lodge being located in the United States.

In 1923 the B'nai B'rith began establishing foundations in American universities known as the B'nai B'rith Hillel Foundations for religious, educational, and social activities among its Jewish students. From the time of Rabbi Benjamin Frankel, the first Hillel director at the University of Illinois to the present, Hillel Foundations extend from the University of Alberta in the Canadian North to the University of Havana in the Caribbean South. However, the Hillel Foundations were not the first campus organizations for as early as 1906 the Menorah Society was founded at Harvard University, coming just eight years after the first Jewish fraternity, the Zeta Beta Tau.

The growth and work of the B'nai B'rith after its one hundredth birthday almost doubled. During the first two years of American participation in World War II, it sold $162,000,000 worth of war bonds. In addition, the order took an active part in providing blood donors and shared in the National War Fund Drive. That service brought to the B'nai B'rith the first citations made by both the Army and Navy to any civilian agency in the country.

38. THE FIRST JEWISH PUBLISHING HOUSE IN AMERICA

In the colonial days, our Jewish communities were small and scattered and the demand for Jewish books was slight and easily satisfied by importations from abroad. As the immigration of Jews from Germany grew, and as the children of the newcomers accepted the English language as their mother tongue, the need for books in English dealing with the Jewish religion, history, and literature began to be felt, less perhaps by the ordinary American Jew than by the rabbis and those concerned with education.

The first attempt to fill the need for publishing Jewish books was made in the city of Cincinnati in 1854, by Rabbi Isaac Mayer Wise and his brother-in-law Edward Bloch, who practically unaided founded the printing and publishing firm called the Bloch Publishing Company. It began by publishing the early Jewish periodicals in this country, (see Ch. 31) among them "American Israelite," "The Chicago Israelite," and "The Reform Advocate." The impulse which brought these periodicals into being grew out of a genuine fear of the Christian missionary societies and their free literature. The Jewish religion was in danger because there were no Jewish books. Rabbi Wise and Mr. Bloch, therefore, felt it necessary to confound the missionary work, save the younger Jewish generation, develop a group of young American Jewish writers, and try to bring unity to a religiously discordant Jewish world through the creation and development of common literary interests.

In the early '60's the Bloch firm undertook the publication of prayerbooks, Bibles, and Hebrew and English textbooks for religious schools. Notable as being the first Hebrew prayer book to be published in America was the "Minhag America" which contained prayers in Hebrew, German and English for the High Holidays edited by Rabbi Wise for Reform Congregations. In later years there appeared liturgical works as the "Sabbath Festival and Holy Day Prayer Book" for Conservative use and the "Standard Prayer Book" and "Standard Machzor" for Orthodox use. Then came the publication of the famous Leeser Bible, the first English translation in this country.

These were the early stages of the Bloch Publishing Company. Then it expanded when the late Charles E. Bloch, son of the founder transferred the business to New York City in 1901. Known as the "Dean of Jewish Publishers in America," he was responsible for the development and high reputation of his firm. To him goes the credit for having spread the printed word among Jews in all walks of life.

The firm which boasts the country's finest collection of Judaica and Hebraica continues today under the leadership of his younger son, Edward H. Bloch, who was associated with his father for many years. The company has become known as an "Otzar Hasefarim" a "Treasury of Jewish Books." The Bloch imprint covers every branch of Judaism. There are textbooks of every description to meet the various types of curricula. Foremost are such subjects as Bible, liturgy, music, biography, history, theology, rabbinics, and current problems. The list also includes juvenile and adult fiction, drama, poetry, as well as a famous cook book featuring Jewish recipes of which more than 150,000 copies have been sold.

The companies bi-monthly "Book Bulletin" edited by Anna Fisch, and its vice-president, Solomon Kerstein, first published in 1929 has become an indispensable medium of information to Jews and non-Jews alike. It is the only bibliographic bi-monthly of Jewish books in English, Hebrew and Yiddish which serves as a guide to the Jewish book lover. In addition to the "Book Bulletin" which the company distributes free the world over, it also issues periodically various Jewish and Hebraic catalogues and selected book lists.

The year 1954 marks the tercentenary of the Jewish community in America and the centenary of the Bloch Company, its oldest Jewish publishing firm.

39. THE FIRST JEWISH PHILANTHROPIST IN AMERICA

Judah Touro, the son of Rabbi Isaac Touro, the first minister of the Newport Rhode Island Congregation (see Ch. 88), was the earliest and most generous of American Jewish philanthropists and civic benefactors. His extensive fortune was largely accumulated by mercantile, shipping and other activities in New Orleans.

He was born in 1775 at Newport, arriving coincidentaly with the outbreak of the American Revolution. Even his death paralleled a great historic period. He died four years after the Compromise of 1850, at the venerable age of seventy-nine.

When Judah was eight years old his father died and four years later his mother passed away. Judah and a brother and sister, Abraham and Rebecca, became the wards of an uncle, the well-known Moses Michael Hays of Boston. Here, he learned at an early age, that one could be a devout Jew and yet mingle freely with his Christian brethren, teaching them to respect his faith, while at the same time respecting theirs. After having been forbidden to marry his childhood sweetheart, Catherine Hays, his cousin, he departed for New Orleans where he is said to have been the first Jewish settler. Groomed for business, there he put into practice the business theories of his twenty-eight years. With full confidence in his abilities, he opened a store and dispensed "Yankee notions."

Patriotically, when the War of 1812 broke out, he enlisted in the army and fought under General Andrew Jackson. When struck by a cannon ball, wounded and left for dying in the Battle of New Orleans, the most decisive battle of the war, he was fortunate enough to be picked up by Rezen David Shepard, and treated in time. After the war, he returned to private life and continued as before. In a short time he became wealthy.

In 1802 when Touro arrived in New Orleans, it was a straggling Spanish-French village; at the time of his death, it had become a great city and he played a conspicuous part in its transformation. He built the first free library in New Orleans, which was the first free library in the world; founded the Touro Infirmary, one of the South's best hospitals; and erected the Shakespeare Alms House for the poor. The Touro Synagogue and Touro Street all perpetuate his name in New Orleans.

In his will his many bequests to institutions of all denominations all over the world continued the philanthropy which he practiced during his life. He left from two thousand to five thousand dollars to every synagogue in America then in existence. Hebrew schools, hospitals, and relief societies in America and Palestine also received help through his will. The money which he left for the Mount Sinai Hospital enabled it to complete its first building. To the legislature of the State of Rhode Island he left a trust fund for the support of the rabbi of the Newport Synagogue. To carry on the charitable work of Moses Montifiore in Palestine, he left the unheard of sum of $50,000. During his lifetime, he had bought and freed many slaves. He had also

(*Courtesy of the American Jewish Historical Society*)
Judah Touro
1775-1854

63

donated a church building to a New Orleans Christian congregation.

Thanks to his liberal contribution of $10,000 a monument was erected at the site of the first battle of the Revolutionary War, at Bunker Hill. When this, the first public monument in America was dedicated, he was paid special homage by Daniel Webster who made a great speech.

Truly then did he earn the ephithet inscribed on his tombstone:

"By righteousness and integrity he collected his wealth,
In charity and for salvation he dispensed it.
The last of his name, he inscribed it in the book of philanthropy
To be remembered forever."

40. THE FIRST JEWISH HOSPITAL IN AMERICA

On June 5, 1855, the first Jewish hospital in America known as "The Jews' Hospital" was completed at a cost of $35,000 and took in its first patient. The building was located on Twenty-eighth Street near Seventh Avenue in Lower Manhattan and stood where a tomato patch once grew and where people were accustomed to build bon-fires. The hospital was founded almost single-handed by a remarkable man, an American Jew who bore the name of Sampson Simson.

A hundred years ago New York like the rest of the country was growing rapidly, and was suffering from growing pains. Many of the new immigrants who were constantly pouring in from Europe had to live in crowded, unhealthy slums, and the rate of illness rose to alarming proportions. City hospitals like Bellevue existed, but for the Jewish community this was not enough. The erection of a hospital, an institution sponsored by the Jewish community itself was a project everyone had been discussing for a long time and doing nothing about. It was then that Sampson Simson, a man of plans who had already lived a long, colorful life, came forward and with one bold stroke broke through all the difficulties.

The Jews' Hospital—Mt. Sinai Hospital (1855-1872 Building)

Simson had taken a life-long interest in communal affairs, and no cause ever appealed to him in vain regardless of creed. Combined with this he was an observant Jew, who had even baked his own matzos for Passover at home. In 1880 he had delivered an address in Hebrew when he was graduated from Columbia University, the first Jew to receive a degree from that institution. He was one of the first Americans to donate sums of money for Jerusalem charities. Finally one wintry day in 1852, he called upon his good friends, all leaders of the Shearith Israel Synagogue, to hear his plan for a Jews' Hospital.

The idea was very simple, but no one had ever thought of it before. Ignoring all existing societies, he wished to enroll members at five dollars a year; these members would elect trustees to guide the hospital. A group of young people had promised to run a ball and raise a thousand dollars; he himself would provide the land on which to build the hospital. The community accepted the plan wholeheartedly, incorporation papers were drawn up, and Sampson Simson was elected its first president.

The new hospital grew with the mushrooming of the city itself. In 1866, to make it clear that it served the community without distinction of race or religion, it changed its name to "The Mount Sinai Hospital." Today its staff includes almost nine hundred physicians and its facilities are the best that are known to medical research. Its seventeen buildings stretch along Fifth Avenue for three crowded city blocks and it is still expanding. In 1948 it treated 15,514 patients in its private wards and aided almost a quarter of a million people in its out-patient department.

41. THE FIRST JEWISH COMMODORE IN AMERICA

Uriah Phillips Levy, one of the most colorful figures in American naval history, is America's first Jewish commodore.

This hard headed, bold adventurer was born in Philadelphia, became a cabin boy at ten, and spent most of his years as a

Commodore Uriah Phillips Levy

sailor before the mast, or as an officer on merchant vessels in the navy.

When the War of 1812 broke out, he immediately volunteered for service and was commissioned as Sailing Master in the United States Navy. Until 1813 he served on the ship "Alert." Then he went on the brig "Argus" which captured several prizes. Uriah Levy was placed in command of one, but the prize was recaptured by the English and Levy and the crew were kept as prisoners for sixteen months in England. After his release, his heroism and daring gained him one promotion after the other.

In 1816 he was made Sailing Master on the "Franklin 74," a much coveted position. The fact of this promotion made much trouble for him. Unjustly accused of failing in his duty, he was court-martialed and dropped from the list as Captain. But Levy fought back, and a Court of Inquiry appointed by Congress was so impressed by his story, that he was restored to the navy with the rank of Captain. In 1860 his complete loyalty and efficiency as an officer was proved and he was promoted to the rank of Commodore. As Commodore, he was one of the first individuals to fight against the barbarous practice of flogging on the high seas, which finally culminated in the passing of a law abolishing forever corporal punishment in the United States Navy.

Levy was so ardent an admirer of Thomas Jefferson that he donated a statue of the president which now stands in Statuary Hall in the Capitol in Washington. For many years he was the owner of and preserved Jefferson's beautiful home in Monticello, on a magnificent hill, just above the University of Virginia which is now a government memorial.

Uriah Levy, valiant and determined, died in New York in 1862, shortly before the outbreak of the Civil War. He offered his entire fortune to President Lincoln for his country's use, proving that he was as humane as he was brave.

On March 28, 1943, the U. S. S. Levy, a destroyer-escort, was named in his honor and launched at Port Newark, N. J.

42. THE FIRST AMERICAN FLAG
WITH HEBREW LETTERS

When Abraham Lincoln took up his residence in Washington
to assume the office of President of the United States, he received a flag of our country bearing upon its silken folds a
Hebrew quotation from the first chapter of the Book of Joshua:
"Have I not commanded thee? Be strong and of good courage;
be not afraid, neither be thou dismayed; for the Lord thy
God is with thee withersoever thou goest."

The man who sent this gift was Abraham Kohn, a merchant
and later city clerk of Chicago. Mr. Kohn, like the majority of
the Jews in the United States was a strong supporter of Abraham
Lincoln in his fight for the emancipation of the Negro slaves.
Because of his militant Republicanism, Kohn was widely known
in the Democratic press as "one of the blackest Republicans,"
and he was in the forefront of every political activity. It was
during the presidential campaign of 1860 that Kohn met Lincoln.
Shortly after the Republican National Convention of that year,
at which Lincoln won the nomination, he made a tour of
Chicago to meet important Republican leaders and to lay the
groundwork for the campaign.

Kohn's popularity and influence were brought to Lincoln's
attention by his advisors who recognized in the Jewish merchant an ally whose acquaintance would prove a valuable asset
in the coming election. Lincoln was introduced to Kohn by
Congressman Isaac N. Arnold who took him to Kohn's store.
It was this meeting that inspired Kohn with a feeling of admiration for the distinguished visitor and a conviction that he was
the destined American Moses and freer of the slaves who were
kept in bondage.

This found expression in sending to Lincoln shortly after
his election, a silk American flag, the work of his own hands,
with Hebrew letters from the first chapter of Joshua painted
in colors along the folds.

In appreciation of this unique gift, Lincoln wrote to Kohn
to thank him and although the letter has been lost, the following
tribute was paid Mr. Kohn in a speech of President McKinley
made in 1885: "Could anything have given Lincoln more cheer

or been better calculated to sustain his courage or strengthen his faith in the mighty work before him?" Thus commanded and thus assured, Lincoln journeyed to the capitol where he took the oath to office and registered an oath in Heaven, an oath to save the Union. And the Lord was with him until every oath was kept."

43.   THE FIRST PEDIATRIC CLINIC IN AMERICA

Today spread all over the country are hundreds of pediatric clinics that treat thousands of children. Hundreds of doctors learn, practice, and teach in them. But it was not until 1861 that the first pediatric clinic in this country, was established. In that year Dr. Abraham Jacobi, a Jewish physician, opened the parent clinic.

Dr. Jacobi was born in 1830 at Hartum, Westphalia. When he was eighteen years old he was imprisoned for his participation in the German Revolution of 1848. He settled in New York in 1853, and only a year after his arrival in this country, attracted the attention of the medical profession with the invention of the laryngoscope. From then on, for over a period of forty-two years he was connected with numerous hospitals in New York and taught pediatrics in the various New York medical schools. He made many significant contributions to the field of infant feeding and inaugurated the first medical bedside instruction in America.

When Columbia University's College of Physicians and Surgeons appointed Jacobi as professor of infant pathology and therapeutics, the first systemized instruction in the field began. It was upon this appointement that the clinical and scientific aspects of pediatrics in this country had its starting point.

Dr. Jacobi was the first doctor in America to recognize the importance of boiling cow's milk for infant feeding and persistently recommended it as early as 1877. When diphtheria anti-toxin was discovered, he was one of the first doctors in America to apply it in practice.

He died at an advanced age after a stirring life as practitioner, teacher, author, and outstanding figure in American medical circles.

His chief work is the Collectania Jacobi which was published in 1909.

44. THE FIRST JEWISH CHAPLAIN IN AMERICA

Thousands upon thousands of Jewish refugees had crossed the Atlantic to help build a life of freedom for all. Now in America, they found a nation in chains. They rallied behind Lincoln to help make America the land of the free, for white men and black men alike.

As soon as the Civil War broke out, Congress passed, on July 22, 1861, the act establishing the national defense and it was provided that each regiment should have a chaplain, as was the custom heretofore, to be appointed by the commander on a vote of the field officers and company. It further provided that "the chaplain so appointed must be a regular ordained minister of the Christian denomination."

This gave rise to widespread comment and agitation which was taken up by the newspapers and many public patriotic societies. The then recently organized Board of Delegates of American Israelites presented to President Lincoln, and both to the Senate and House of Representatives, a memorial setting forth the facts that the Acts of Congress "be formally amended, so that there shall be no discrimination as against professors of the Jewish faith, in the several laws affecting the appointment of Chaplains in the service of the United States."

Rabbi Arnold Fischel of Congregation Shearith Israel of New York, backed by the authority of the Board went to Washington to point out the need to President Lincoln and was most instrumental in bringing about the change in the law. In the meantime, without official recognition, he took it upon himself the duty of visiting camps and hospitals, ministering to the needs of Jewish soldiers.

On May 20, 1862, the law was changed to include rabbis and thereupon President Lincoln appointed Rabbi Jacob Frankel of Philadelphia as the first Jewish chaplain. This appointment was followed by that of two others — Rabbi B. H. Gotthelf of Louisville and Rabbi Ferdinand Sarner of New York who immediately entered upon the discharge of their respective duties. No Jewish regimental chaplains, however, were appointed during the war.

In the Spanish American War the question of chaplains did not arise as the war was comparatively short.

During World War I six Jewish chaplains were appointed and the president for the first time was authorized to appoint a regimental chaplain. Rabbi Elkan C. Voorsanger was thereupon appointed the first Jewish regimental chaplain by President Wilson. Since he was already abroad as a volunteer with a hospital unit, he received his commission there, on November 24, 1917. He held the first Passover services in the war zone, at St. Nazaire, in 1918 — the first Jewish holiday celebration officially conducted by an officer of the United States Army.

Ultimately twelve rabbis saw active service as regimental chaplains, ten of them abroad. Thirteen others were commissioned First Lieutenant Chaplains and served in camps and cantonments with the army in the United States.

During World War II the number of Jewish Army and Navy chaplains reached three hundred and eleven.

45. THE FIRST DRUGSTORE IN AMERICA

There were no drugstores in America as we know them for many years. But in 1864 Dr. David de Leon, a Jewish physician from Charleston, South Carolina, opened America's first drugstore.

Anyone walking into his store would find that it was a scientific pharmacy where doctor's prescriptions were compounded. There were on powder puffs, razor blades, ice cream sodas or coca cola bottles to be seen.

Dr. de Leon, the "father of the modern drugstore," was one of the most famous Jewish officers of the Mexican War. On two occasions he took the place of commanding officers who had been put out of action and acted with such gallantry and ability as to merit expressions of gratitude from Congress. In the Battle of Chapultepec he is credited with having led cavalry charges into the cannon's mouth and won the sobriquet "the fighting doctor," and was advanced to the rank of Surgeon-General of the Union forces.

As a southerner, at the outbreak of the Civil War, he resigned from the Union Army and was appointed first Surgeon-General of the Confederacy.

From the small beginnings of Dr. de Leon's store, drugstore retail trade has grown to its present size and has come to include among the merchandise it offers for sale thousands of products of modern civilization.

46. THE FIRST JEWISH STATESMAN IN AMERICA

Although sympathies of the Jewish population as a whole was with the North when the seething ferment between the North and South burst into the flame of the Civil War, Jews also gave signal service to the Confederacy. Judah P. Benjamin was the outstanding Jew in the South's struggle and held three successive posts in the Confederate Cabinet before he was finally appointed Secretary of State. His loyalty to the system of slavery surprised Jews and Christians alike. One northern preacher who knew the devotion of the Jews to freedom and justice, called Mr. Benjamin "an Israelite with an Egyptian heart."

Judah P. Benjamin was born in the West Indies, then in the possession of England. His family migrated to Charleston, South Carolina, shortly after the War of 1812. Young Benjamin received an early education there and at the age of fourteen entered Yale College and won high distinction as a scholar. Early in 1828, before having graduated from college, he arrived in New Orleans, there obtained work in a business concern, and began studying law at night. At the age of twenty-one, he was admitted to the Louisiana Bar, and in a short time won a high reputation in the legal field. Subsequently he entered politics and in 1845 was elected member of the convention held to revise the constitution of his state. His ability as a jurist became recognized both nationally and internationally, and President Pierce tendered him the position of Associate Justice of the Supreme Court of the United States. He preferred politics, however, and in 1852 was elected by Louisiana to the United States Senate and was reelected six years later.

With the slavery issue in the forefront, Benjamin upheld the issue as well as the principle of State Sovereignty. Like many Southerners, he long resisted secession, but when the step was taken, he cast his lot with the Confederacy. His former colleague in the Senate, Jefferson Davis appointed him Attorney-General of the Confederacy, Secretary of War, and finally Secretary of State. Benjamin was the President's most trusted advisor and was often referred to as "the brains of the Confederacy."

When the Confederate forces suffered one crushing defeat after another, Benjamin was made the scapegoat. At the end of the war, penniless, and over fifty, he found his way to London. Here he was befriended by Disraeli and Gladstone. He once again resumed the practice of law, and began writing law books which brought him a fortune. His book on "Sales" is still recognized as authoritative in law schools. He made an income of $100,000 a year, and was acknowledged as one of the leading barristers of England, and became one of the first American Jews to hold the title of "King's Councellor." The very first dinner ever given in honor of an American by the Bar of England was tendered for Benjamin upon his retirement.

47. THE FIRST JEW
TO RECEIVE THE CONGRESSIONAL MEDAL OF HONOR

Hundreds of Jewish soldiers gave their lives for the cause of Negro emancipation. Many led campaigns of men against the Southern forces. For centuries the Jew had fought for their own freedom. They were happy now to protect others against oppression.

Four Jews attained the rank of general officer in the Union army. The highest ranking individual of them all was Frederick Knefler of Indianapolis, an immigrant Jew born in Hungary, who volunteered as a private soldier in his home town of Indianapolis and rose to be colonel of the 79th Indiana regiment. His highest actual rank was Brigadier General, to which the temporary rank of Brevet Major General was later added.

Three Jews were full colonels and brevetted brigadier general; Edward S. Solomon of Chicago, Leopold Blumberg of Baltimore, and Philip J. Joachimson of New York, who as district attorney in New York City had secured the first conviction for the inhuman traffic in slaves.

On July 12, 1862, for the first time in American history, Congress authorized the awarding of the Congressional Medal of Honor, the highest honor that can be given to an American soldier, and the most difficult to obtain. Seven Jews won the Congressional Medal of Honor, the first one in 1864 going to Sgt. Leopold Karpeles.

Karpeles, who was born in Prague in 1838, had come to the United States at the age of twelve. Soon after his arrival, he joined his brother in Texas whose business was conveying caravans across the Mexican border. When the Civil War broke out, he enlisted in the army in Springfield, Massachusetts. He was awarded the Congressional Medal of Honor for his act in rallying the men of the 57th Massachusetts Volunteers around the flag and turning a retreat into a victory. The official citation read: "At the Battle of the Wilderness, May 6, 1864, while color bearer of his regiment, he rallied the retreating troops and induced them to check the advance of the enemy."

Much later, during World War I this distinction was continued among the Jewish soldiers. Nine governments heaped awards upon Sgt. Benjamin Kaufman who fought so valorously at Argonne and his own country gave him the Congressional Medal of Honor. For many years he served as National Commander of the Jewish War Veterans in the United States.

48. THE FIRST HEBREW COLLEGES IN AMERICA

The need for a school to train rabbi's, hazzanim, and Hebrew teachers was not keenly felt in America until the 1840's and 1850's. Rarely did a child attend school beyond the age of thirteen which marked the year of confirmation, and the year in which a boy gave up his formal studies and became apprenticed to a trade or worked in a business establishment. Many ministers who were engaged in various congregations were not strictly rabbis, but more than usually, laymen self-taught. In New York, Mordecai Manuel Noah and S. M. Isaacs, made constant mention of the need of a college of higher Jewish learning. In 1852 Sampson Simson tried to organize a Jewish Theological Seminary and Scientific Institute. However, it never progressed beyond the planning stage because Simson was too busy with other organizations that he fostered. (See Ch. 40).

Isaac Leeser, a self-taught German rabbi of the Congregation Mikveh Israel, who had seen the need of higher Jewish education in America and had long harped on the subject in the "Occident" which he founded, opened the first institution for the rabbinate and other higher Hebrew learning in Philadelphia on October 25, 1867. Maimonides College, as it was so called was maintained by the Hebrew Educational Society of Philadelphia and the Board of Delegates of American Israelites. Among the faculty members were included Marcus M. Jastrow and Sabato Morais, while Leeser served as president. Leeser died three months after the college opened, but it carried on until 1873, when lack of funds forced it to close its doors. Five students comprised its first class, three of whom occupied pulpits.

The first Hebrew teachers' training school in the United States was established in Philadelphia in 1897 in pursuance of the will of Hyman Gratz, of the famous early American family of merchants and civic leaders. Gratz bequeathed a sum of approximately $150,000 to Congregation Mikveh Israel in trust for establishing a college "for the education of Jews residing in the city and county of Philadelphia." It was thought at first that he had intended to project a general college, but since funds were insufficient, Dr. Cyrus Adler of the Smithsonian Institute in Washington suggested that it become an institute in the training of teachers for Jewish religious schools.

In order to provide a theological center from which the beliefs and tenants of Reform Judaism might be disseminated, Rabbi Isaac M. Wise in 1875 founded the Hebrew Union College in Cincinnati and served as its president until 1900. The first graduation was held on July 11, 1883 at which time Israel Aaron, Henry Berkowitz, Joseph Kranskopt and David Philipson were ordained. The College has five beautiful buildings on a fine campus and is located near the University of Cincinnati. Although it still maintains this branch, in 1949 it became affiliated with the Jewish Institute of Religion in New York which was founded by Rabbi Stephen Wise. (See Ch. 73).

In 1886, Sabato Morais founded the Jewish Theological Seminary of America in New York. Its function was to train rabbis and teachers along the lines of Conservative Judaism. In 1902 under the leadership of Solomon Schecter, former Reader of Rabbinics at Cambridge University, London and discoverer of the Cairo Genizah, the Jewish Theological Seminary became one of the greatest schools of its kind in the world and was popularly called Schecter's Seminary. One of its graduates, Joseph H. Hertz, became the chief rabbi of the British Empire.

Higher Hebrew education in this country received a further impetus when in 1907, Moses Aaron Dropsie left $1,000,000 to found Dropsie College in Philadelphia for "the promotion of and instruction in Hebrew and cognate languages and their respective literatures without student discrimination and without any theological basis." Dr. Cyrus Adler served as its first president.

Most of the leaders of American Orthodox Jewry are provided by the Isaac Elchanan Theological Seminary in New York whose guiding spirit was Dr. Bernard Revel until the time of his death in 1941 (see Ch. 85) and the Hebrew Theological College in Chicago whose president is Rabbi Saul Silver. In 1928 the Isaac Elchanan Theological Seminary established Yeshiva College, the first Jewish sponsored college of liberal arts and sciences in the history of the diaspora. In 1945 the

New York State Board of Regents conferred university rank upon Yeshiva College and it became the first American univer-. sity under Jewish auspices.

In 1950 the New York State Board of Regents granted Yeshiva University a charter permitting the establishment of a Medical School. This will mark the first medical school under Jewish auspices in the entire history of Diaspora Jewry.

49.   THE FIRST AMERICAN JEWISH SCULPTOR IN THE IMPERIAL ACADEMY

The nineteenth century was hardly an era propitious for the fine arts. America, still a fairly young country in which first of all forests had to be cleared, houses erected, railroads built, and rivers spanned, there was no time for leisure. Strangely enough there lived at that time a Jewish sculptor of international renown, Moses Jacob Ezekiel, who not only made pretty statues but perpetuated in bronze, marble, and clay, the beauty and noble aspirations of mankind as well as its ugliness and vicissitudes. His unusually distinguished career as artist included several international medals, and the honor of knighthood both from the king of Italy and the emperor of Germany. In 1872, the highest honor that can befall an artist was bestowed upon him, when he had the distinct privilege of being accepted as a full pledged member in the world-famous Imperial Academy of Arts in Rome. He was the first American and the first Jew to receive such a distinction.

Ezekiel was born in Richmond, Virginia, in 1844. As a young boy he attended the Virginia Military Academy and showed great talent in drawing. When the Civil War broke out, he volunteered in the Confederate Army and served throughout the war. He then went abroad to study sculpture, won a prize which took him to Rome for further study, and lived there most of his life in a luxurious modern studio which he installed in the ancient Tower of Belisarius.

His works were exhibited in many art salons of many European cities. For one of his earlier works, his bas relief "Israel" he was awarded the Michel Baer Prize of Rome. American history was another of his favorite subjects. It was in recognition of his colossal bust of George Washington that the Imperial Academy accepted him into their fold. His best known work from the Jewish point of view is the "Statue of Religious Liberty" which he made in 1876 for the B'nai B'rith to present as part of their centennial exposition. It stands in Fairmount Park, Philadelphia.

Another American Jewish sculptor of note, Jo Davidson, who was born in New York in 1883 and been dubbed the "Biographer in Bronze" has modeled more noted people than any other contemporary sculptor. Some of his works are of Presidents Wilson, Roosevelt, and Truman, and have earned him the title of "Dean of United States Sculptors."

50. THE FIRST JEWISH ORCHESTRA CONDUCTOR

New York today has one of the finest symphony orchestras in the world under the best conductors, the excellent Julliard School of Music, many other musical organizations, and much popular interest in music. Throughout the nineteenth century interest in music was growing, but its first symphony orchestra was not formed until 1873.

In 1871 Leopold Damrosch, a Prussian Jew, came to New York, and was one of the first good teachers of music. With a small circle of friends who liked music, mostly amateurs, Damrosch formed an "Oratorio Society." On Saturday evenings they met in the music hall of Damrosch's house and when the group got larger in Pythian Hall. They did choral singing and played symphonies and other music of the time for their own enjoyment. Damrosch led the group and he himself played the violin.

Damrosch and his friends also formed the New York Symphony Society in 1873, the first organized group in New York devoted only to symphonic music. The society gave hundreds of concerts down to 1926 and did much to raise the standards of and gain appreciation for good music.

It was as conductor of the New York Symphony Society that Walter Johannas Damrosch, the son of Leopold Damrosch, earned for himself the title of "Dean of American Conductors" after inheriting the baton from his father. Now for the first time in America, music of great composers was brought to towns and villages where it was never before heard of. The son was also responsible for the first American performances of many great works and was the first American conductor to go on a tour of European cities.

51.   THE FIRST "ONE PRICE" STORE IN AMERICA

Jews have taken part in making American business synonymous with enterprise and achievement. Such a Jew was David Lubin, a dreamer and enthusiast who forgot himself in one great cause after the other.

In 1855 at the age of six, David Lubin was brought to New York by his immigrant parents. At the age of twelve he left school and went to work. The adventurous youngster was a strong supporter of Lincoln who represented his own ideals and hopes. When the Civil War broke out he ran away to sea and tried to join the army. At twenty-five he made a trip across the continent and landed in Sacramento, California, which at the time, although the state capitol, was still a rough mining camp.

Above a basement saloon, Lubin started a little store under a sign "D. Lubin — ONE PRICE." Here, for the first time in America, he established the principle of selling merchandise at retail with fixed prices marked in plain figures on each individual item. In a short while he won everyone's respect for his honesty and fair dealing, and The Mechanic's Store as it came to be called became a Sacramento institution. By 1874, he had established and advertised several business principles which today represent fundamental precepts of retailing, but which then were startlingly new: (1) to sell at one price only; (2) to mark all merchandise with the selling price in plain figures; (3) never to represent merchandise; (4) to buy or manufacture goods at the lowest price possible: (5) to figure out at how low a profit the goods could be sold. The enterprise became not only the largest retail store in Sacramento, but later added a San Francisco store.

As his business grew and people from far and near came to buy from him, he solved the broader problem of transportation by establishing for the first time in America the mail order house. The development of the mail order house from that time on and especially as expanded by the great philanthropist, Julius Rosenwald, the head of the Sears Roebuck Company, is the saga of the modernization of rural life. Hardly an item for personal or general use is omitted today from the huge catalogue which the firm distributes annually to over forty million people.

In 1884, Lubin made a journey to Palestine. He always considered it the turning point of his career. Upon his return to America, his interest in business shifted to farming. He began to study soils and methods by which California farmers could best raise products for the market, a study he felt could apply in the rebirth of Palestine. He soon became the owner of the largest fruit packing company in the state and founder of California's Fruit Growers' Exchange. At this time he was also one of the early sponsors of cheap parcel post.

Convinced of the idea that the consumer could buy food more cheaply and farmers could get more by-products through cooperation on a world-wide basis, he founded the International Institute for Agriculture. Nation after nation saw the feasibility of his plan and forty-five countries joined in what was the first permanent internation cooperation in the world, the precursor of the League of Nations.

Lubin was appointed first United States representative to the Institute and continued in this post for ten years. The King of Italy, Victor Emanual III gave a splendid building for its use. Nations sent their official representatives and technical experts to cooperate with Lubin who worked equally for the American farmer and the common man the world over.

On January 1, 1919, David Lubin died in Rome at the age of seventy, overflowing to the last with fiery enthusiasm, never ceasing his untiring labors for his cause.

52.   THE FIRST "Y" UNDER JEWISH AUSPICES IN AMERICA

The first "Y" under Jewish auspices in America was organized in New York in March, 1874, exactly thirty years after the world "Y" movement began in London as a desperate attempt to combat the terrible poverty and vice of the Industrial Revolution.

The following words marked the birth of the organization: "WE, the UNDERSIGNED, desiring to promote harmony and good fellowship among Hebrew young men and to unite them in an organization tending to improve their social, moral and mental condition, do form an association under the name and style of the "Young Men's Hebrew Association.""

The first meeting was held at the home of Dr. Simeon Newton Leo who was the moving force in the formation of the new organization. His residence was located at 320 West 33 Street, and meetings were held there week after week until the number of persons attending necessitated more adequate quarters. For a while the meetings took place at the Thirty-fourth Street Synagogue and then in the Trustees room of Temple Emanuel until a small room was rented at 112 West 21st Street. Here an extended program of education and recreation was inaugurated and many new members were enrolled.

In 1886, a small building was rented at 721 Lexington Avenue near 58th Street. Here the activities of the Association were carried on for nine years. From the very beginning and throughout this formative period, the progam, in addition to the social, recreational and club activities, stressed the Jewish interests which gave prestige and support to the institution.

The infant organization was nurtured with infinite care by men of prominence in the professional and business life of New York City, including Oscar S. Straus who had served in the cabinets of four United States Presidents. On May 3, 1874 a constitution was adopted and officers and directors were elected. The first permanent officers to be chosen were: President Lewis May; Vice-President, Dr. S. Newton Leo; Treasurer, Sol B. Solomon; Secretary, Julius J. Frank.

The movement received its greatest impetus from the well-known philanthropist, Jacob Schiff. He had hardly been in this country barely more than a decade when he became a member of the YMHA Board because he saw in its program among other things, promise of Jewish educational awakening among the youth of the city. In 1898 Schiff presented it with its first permanent home. This structure on Lexington Avenue and 65th Street, provided the YMHA with club and classrooms, a library and gymnasium. So impressed was Schiff with the growth of the YMHA and its service to the Jewish community that before the year was over he announced a gift of a much larger building on the corner of Lexington Avenue and 92nd Street, an address which was destined to become world famous. The movement grew and spread by leaps and bounds to other states.

In 1882, the Association established a downtown New York branch, the first Jewish neighborhood center for immigrant groups. The first building that was owned and erected by a YMHA, was dedicated by the Dallas, Texas YMHA in 1887.

In 1902 the Young Women's Hebrew Association was founded by public spirited women who recognized the need for a Center for Jewish working girls and students. The moving spirit of this effort was Mrs. Israel Unterberg, in whose home meetings were held at regular intervals.

The first attempt to organize a national association of YMHA's was the American Hebrew Association, which was formed in 1880 and lasted until 1883. By the year 1907 there were more than one hundred YMHA's with a membership of 20,000. The time was ripe for regional organization and in 1910 five regional YMHA associations came into being.

The first permanent national organization of Jewish Community Centers and YMHA's was the National Council of YMHA's and Kindred Associations formed in 1913. Among its founders were Louis Marshall, Jacob Schiff, Felix Warburg, Dr. Mordecai Kaplan, Harry Fischel, Dr. Cyrus Adler, Judah L. Magnus, Samuel Goldsmith, now executive director of the Jewish Charities of Chicago and I. Edwin Goldwasser. It was the merger in 1921 of this Council with the warborn National Jewish Welfare Board that established the Jewish Welfare Board as we now know of it.

Today a dynamic force in American Jewish life, the "Y" serves over 500,000 children, young people and adults in more than two hundred communities for the fulfillment of Jewish life and the advancement of society as a whole.

53. THE FIRST YIDDISH POET IN AMERICA

Yankel Zvi Sobel who published his first long poem in 1876 which depicted the lives of recently arrived immigrants is considered the first Yiddish poet in America, though Yiddish verse had been written here before his time.

It was not until the year 1870 that Yiddish literature as such began in this country. Of the twenty Yiddish writers of verse and story of this period the only one singled out as a writer of literary merit was Sobel.

Yiddish literature in the United States was by no means a continuation of the European current, but a unique growth resulting from specific American conditions. Whereas Yiddish literature in Europe primarily fought mediavalism in Jewish life, Yiddish literature in the United States was brought to life by the new industrial proletariat. The American-Jewish proletariat consisted of immigrants, who like Sobel, had run away from the Czar's pogroms in 1881 and from the despotism which was its aftermath.

This first decade was devoted almost entirely to journalism and not to literature. But a truly progressive Yiddish culture and literature was brought into being by Jewish forces that preached the gospel of social justice, that stood up against social exploitation in the sweatshops, that wept with the sufferers and the ever growing Jewish labor movement. Thus, the first propagandists of social justice and the first singers of labor, of whom first and foremost was Sobel, laid the foundation for Yiddish literature in the United States.

Sobel, who had studied at the world famous Slabotka Yeshiva in Poland, was a keen student of Hebrew and contributed Hebrew verse as well to such outstanding old world periodicals as Smolensky's "Hashachar."

54. THE FIRST TALKING MACHINE INVENTION

To some of us the most wonderful of all the marvelous inventions, of which we have so many in these days, is the talking machine or phonograph, no matter by what name we call it. That a black flat disk coverered with tiny lines should be able to give us the golden voice of Melba or Caruso, the wonderful tones of a violin in the hands of a master, the full crash of a brass band or the winged words of a great orator, seems impossible to believe. Yet we know that it is true.

Scientists had known for a long time that it was possible to make a record of the vibrations of sound; but the first practical instrument to do this was patented by Edison in 1877. By simply reversing this machine, it was found that you could "make it talk." However, early records were not satisfactory.

In the first decade after the Civil War there lived in Washington, D. C., a German Jew by the name of Emile Berliner who had taken courses at Cooper Union College in New York and who was working in the same field. His experiments led to the invention of the gramaphone or the flat disk, the first successful kind of talking machine record and the one most of us know today. At first only one side of this was used but today, with practically all disk records, both sides are employed, doubling the capacity of the record. For his development of the so-called "lateral-cut method" of etching the human voice, he was at a later date awarded the Elliot and Cresson Medal by the Franklin Institute.

In the same way much of the glory that goes to Bell for having invented the telephone should go to Berliner, for it was he who really made it a practical instrument. Bell's invention lacked a practical transmitter since it used magnetic induction and the human voice produced only weak undulating currents. Berliner's invention permitted a clear sound of greater volume and resulted in the increase in distance of communication. This transmitter is used in all our telephones today, and is the precursor of the modern microphone.

Berliner's inventive genius reached out and noticeably affected the domains of many other inventions. He discovered methods of improving the acoustics of buildings; made the mo-

tion picture projector possible; and he added further devices
to the telephone.

The helicopter was the last practical invention to engage his
mind. In 1919 his son actually flew the first workable flying
machine of this type. While it has been said that every American war has been marked by some new invention, even the
Korean War has not yet revealed the full measure of change
that may be wrought by the helicopter.

It was in speaking of him that President Herbert Hoover said:
"The German immigrant boy, Emile Berliner, has become one
of America's most useful citizens."

Emile Berliner died in Washington on August 3, 1928.

55. THE FIRST RED CROSS MEETING IN AMERICA

While the Civil War was being fought, the foundations for
a great international humanitarian movement were being laid
in Geneva, Switzerland. In 1863 a congress of delegates met to
found the International Red Cross. The United States at first
remained aloof from the Red Cross, partly because of the sympathy of the European nations towards the Confederate cause.
During the late 1870's, however, private meetings began to be
held in the homes of private citizens of Washington, D. C., in
anticipation of American adherence to the Red Cross convention.

The principal meeting place was the home of Adolphus
Simeon Solomons, a New York born Jewish publisher who had
become prominent in Washington's communal affairs and its
philanthropic organizations. In May 1881, together with Clara
Barton, he issued a call for volunteers, to come meet in his
home to help organize the American Red Cross. It was here
that a proposal was accepted to incorporate in the District of
Columbia a society known as the American Association of the
Red Cross and the movement in America officially began.

After the United States ratified the Red Cross treaty of 1882,
Solomon was one of the three persons appointed by President
Chester A. Arthur in 1884 to represent this country in the Geneva
Congress. Solomons remained an active member of the organiza-

tion for seventeen years and was elected vice-president.

During the Spanish-American War, with Solomons still a member of the executive board, the American Red Cross was to render important service in ministering to the needs of American soldiers. In subsequent war and domestic disaster relief, it assumed a role that has made it an almost indispensable organization in American life.

In 1917 when the Red Cross adopted a nurses' hospital uniform, it turned to Henry A. Dix, a Russian Jewish immigrant, to design it (see Ch. 68). Then the Dix Red Cross uniform took its place as international insignia, and became recognized in whatever corner of the earth suffering called for the ministering of that noble institution.

In May, 1950, at the sixty-ninth anniversary of the founding of the American Red Cross, it was reported that since its inception it had given $147,000,000 worth of aid to domestic disaster victims. The oulay did not include services rendered to servicemen during both World Wars.

56. THE FIRST AMERICANIZATION CLASSES FOR JEWISH IMMIGRANTS

The lot of the Jew in Czarist Russia was not a very happy one. In 1881 there began a hideous nightmare of oppression, rioting, and bloodshed, as dreadful as the orgies of the Spanish Inquisition. Pogroms broke out wherever there were Jews. Jews were persecuted or expelled and thousands of them fled in the wildest exodus in Jewish history, to Germany, Austria, France, England and Palestine. Between 1881 and 1910, 1,562,800 Russian and Polish Jews came to the United States. The same illiberal treatment befell the Jews in Galicia, Rumania, and Austria-Hungary, and from these countries as well came hundreds of thousands of refugees.

The problem of the Jewish community arising from the influx of these refugees in the early 80's became intense because of the lack of existing societies capable of coping with the situation.

In 1882, the Young Men's Hebrew Association of New York

established a downtown branch, the first Jewish neighborhood center for immigrant groups. The rooms were located at 244 East Broadway, but within a year the Y moved to 206 East Broadway, where a new building had been erected for the Hebrew Free School Association. The activities conducted here included for the first time, Americanization classes, English for foreigners and related subjects. One of the teachers was Emma Lazarus, the famous poetess, whose immortal words are inscribed on the base of the Statue of Liberty. The work conducted for the immigrants inspired Jacob Schiff to refer to the "noble missionary work among the Russians conducted by the YMHA." (see Ch. 52).

Baltimore, Maryland also received many of the refugees. The home of Rabbi Benjamin Szold, one of its prominent rabbis, was constantly filled with the haggard men and women asking for advice. To help the newcomers, his daughter, Henrietta Szold, organized classes to teach the immigrants English and the ideals of democracy, patterning her curriculum after the earlier New York one. In 1898 she rented a room above a store in the cheaper section of town and began classes with thirty pupils. During the first semester more than fifty heads, young and old, often father and son, touched each other over the primer, together learning their A B C. The heart throb of it warmed Henrietta's body on the cold wintry nights in the long rides of the little horsecars from the Baltimore slums to her father's home. Soon others learned about the school and came to join. The superintendent of schools in Baltimore saw that the movement was the answer to a great problem and the public school system throughout the country adopted the program.

The immigrants made their adoption. Their children now grown into adults differed from their fellow Americans only in the traditionally acceptable American differences which leaves to each man the free exercise of his religious convictions.

Fifty years after Henrietta Szold began her Americanization classes, Mayor LaGuardia conferred upon her the "Freedom of the City of New York" and said that it was Americanization work such as hers and that of the YMHA that made possible his own ascent to the mayoralty and had saved America from a new slavery.

Henrietta Szold

57. THE FIRST REAL SETTINGS
ON THE AMERICAN STAGE

Show business in America began almost as soon as American
settlers had time to sit down and see a play. The first American
playbill complete with actors' names was printed for production
in 1752. But the theater had been sporadically active before
this. It grew from infancy into an obstreperous youth, and, in
the past few decades, into a fitful maturity.

Jews are found in great numbers as producers and writers of
plays, actors in vaudeville, drama, and the movies, and builders
and owners of theaters.

Head and shoulders above all pioneers in the American theater are producers like Charles Frohman and David Belasco
who made show business seem very solid by investing their
own wealth (unlike today's producers) in scores of their own
productions. Belasco, in particular, left an indelible mark upon
the American stage with his emphasis on reality. For one production he constructed a complete Childs restaurant on the
stage and actually fried eggs. With his clerical collars, priestly
black raiment and the galaxy of female stars he sponsored,
Belasco set a pattern for The Big Producer, of which the contemporary Hollywood counterparts are pallid copies.

Although born of Jewish parents in San Francisco in 1853,
Belasco was educated in Catholic schools. Of an inherently
romantic and imaginative nature, from his earliest years, he
had been a worker in the theater, an experimenter, who both
as playwright and producer attempted and accomplished what
no other American ever tried to do before. He developed a
technique which made the most of lighting facilities and attempted exact reproductions of real life, a new trend in the
American theater called after him "Belascoism" or "realism"
whereby stage settings were no longer painted but real. The
first play he produced, Bronson Howard's "Young Mrs. Win-
throp" ran for nearly two hundred consecutive performances.
Belasco's own "May Blossom" followed the first play and drove
speculator's tickets up to five dollars each. He introduced
"realism" not only in the series of his plays, but in the acting

of the stars he trained and in the many plays he wrote. Mary Pickford graduated from his school to become America's sweetheart. Another, David Warfield, became one of the leading Jewish actors of his day.

In 1910 Belasco's original play of western life, "The Girl of the Golden West," was made into one of the first operas with an American setting. Its premiere was held at the Metropolitan with Toscanini conducting and Caruso and Amato in the chief roles.

In all Belasco produced four hundred plays, works of some one hundred and twenty-five different authors, including one hundred and fifty dramas of his own.

58.   THE FIRST AMERICAN HOLIDAY INAUGURATED BY A JEW

Labor Day, the first Monday in September, was established as a legal holiday through the efforts of Samuel Gompers, one of the most prominent labor leaders of the last generation, and was first celebrated in New York in 1882.

Gompers, who lived to see his dream of organized labor come true in the land of the free, was born in London in 1850. His parents were of Dutch-Jewish origin and his father was a cigarmaker. Having only had four years of formal education, Gompers entered his father's business at the age of twelve. In 1863, he and his family emigrated to New York and he went to work almost immediately in the cigar-maker trade. Their arrival coincided with the Battle of Gettysburg, an atmosphere of intense patriotism, which coupled with Gomper's faith in labor, was to influence his entire future.

As early as the age of fourteen, Gompers had already joined a cigarmaker's union which was affiliated with the national labor union. Ten years later, after the Panic of 1873, he helped found Local 144, which later made labor history. In 1877, Gompers and his friends, Adolph Strasser and Ferdinand Laurell, led a cigarmakers' strike in protest against unsanitary working conditions. Out of this experience for the first time in American history was born the idea of a united labor front.

In Columbus, Ohio, in 1886, he then formed the nucleus of what was to become the American Federation of Labor out of the remnants of a federation of organized trades and labor unions. He was chosen president of the new group at an annual salary of $1,000. The first great campaign undertaken by the American Federation of Labor was the struggle for an eight hour day. This was eventually won, but more improvements were sought. Gompers then proceeded to arouse the country's consciousness for decent wages for workers, clean shops, and successful arbitration machinery, all of which he felt could best be achieved through the organization of unions.

As a result of Gompers' activity as founder of the American Federation of Labor, the garment and clothing industry, through techniques of mass production and distribution, have made the people of the United States the best dressed nation on the earth. The American worker was lifted from the slough of human despair and hunger to human dignity and hope.

In October 1933, national tribute was paid to the great labor leader when President Roosevelt dedicated the Samuel Gompers Memorial in Washington, D. C. In January 1950, on the occasion of the one hundredth anniversary of the birth of Samuel Gompers, one of the first stamps carrying the picture of a Jew, the Gompers stamp, was issued by the United States Post Office.

59. THE FIRST ZIONIST ORGANIZATION IN AMERICA

Since the destruction of the Second Temple in Jerusalem in the year 70 C.E., Jews have always looked in constant hope and prayer for their return to the city and the land of their birth.

Modern Zionism was actually begun and practical work for the rebuilding of the Jewish National Homeland started when the first Zionist Congress was called by Theodore Herzl in Basle, Switzerland, a little over fifty years ago. Modern Zionism made its first appearance in America almost at the beginning of the world Zionist movement.

The Russian Jew in America was especially fertile soil for the development of this movement. He had the nationalistic sympathy which was reinforced by the Russian pogroms and in addition was building up wealth to support it. In 1883 in New York a Russian Jew founded the first "Hovevai Zion" or "Lovers of Zion" group in America. Even in his student days in New York University's Medical School, Dr. Joseph Bluestone, nourished the dream of Zion rebuilt. There were many other visionaries like him and soon the movement began to grow. In 1889 Dr. Bluestone assumed the editorialship of "Shulamith," the first periodical in America devoted exclusively to the upholding of the nationalistic Jewish viewpoint. Later he was elected vice-president of the Zionist Federation.

The first national conference of representatives of the "Hovevai Zion" from New York, Philadelphia, Boston and Baltimore took place in the spacious study of Professor Richard Gottheil at Columbia University in 1898. Professor Gottheil, a prominent orientalist and archeologist had the distinction of serving as the first president of the Zionist Federation of America as the movement subsequently came to be called. Rabbi Stephen S. Wise, one of the early leaders of the movement was chosen its first secretary and accompanied Professor Gottheil to the Second World Zionist Congress.

The Zionist Federation of America has grown from strength to strength. In 1919 under the leadership of Louis Dembitz Brandeis, the Zionist Organization boasted of a membership of 171,000 and two hundred and seventy local societies were affiliated under its wing. Brandeis headed the American Zionist movement for close to seven years and made tremendous contributions to the world Zionist cause particularly during the years of World War I, when the Jewish communities of Europe faced dissolution and European Zionists were forced to hault their work.

The Zionists of America are now organized in over a dozen national bodies representing various shades of opinion: the General Zionists, including the Zionist Organization of America, Hadassah, the largest Woman's Zionist organization in the world, the B'nai Zion formerly called the Order Sons of Zion, the Women's League for Israel, Masada, Junior Hadassah, Young Judaea, and the Campus Zionist Groups; the Labor Zionists, including the Jewish Socialist Labor Party Poale Zion, the League for Labor Israel, Pioneer Women, Hechalutz and Hashomer Hatzair; and the religious Zionists: the Mizrachi Organization of America, Mizrachi Women's Organization, Junior Mizrachi, B'nai Akiva, Hapoel Hamizrachi and Hashomer Hadati and Noar Mizrachi.

The American government has consistently looked with favor toward the establishment of the Jewish national home and Zionism has been endorsed by every president since Wilson. America is in fact a party of the Palestine Mandate through the American-British Palestine Mandate convention of 1924.

On the fourteenth of May, 1948 with the birth of the Jewish State, new horizons opened up for the Zionist Organization and its institutions. No longer a "State on the way," the Zionist Organization became, rather a faithful ambassador of the Jewish State to the mass of the Jewish people in the Diaspora. The common effort was now concentrated on mass immigration and the rapid absorption of the new comers.

Today the American Jewish community, generously supporting political Zionism and the Israeli funds, has already reaped cultural benefits from the Jewish renaissance in Israel. Educators, community leaders, students and laymen alike, draw inspiration from the builders and pioneers, and from the new values being created in Israel. With the destruction of European Jewry through Hitler's onslaught and the advent of World War II, world Jewry looks to America for the future hope and strength of the Zionist movement.

60.   THE FIRST DEPARTMENT STORE IN AMERICA

Though Jews of German origin had settled in this country in the early eighteenth century, the bulk of German-Jewish immigrants migrated to the United States in the period from 1840 to 1860. These Jews were born merchants, buyers, sellers and traders. They loved commerce and the clash of wits. They started their lives in the new country as peddlers. Their hard work, enterprising spirit and ability to organize soon won for them a place of prominence in the life of the growing nation. Soon they gave up the peddlers pack and became shop-keepers.

One of this group of immigrants was a humble peddler from the province of Bavaria by the name of Lazarus Straus who was to become the father of the three most famous brothers in American Jewish history, Nathan, Oscar, and Isadore, and with whom the story of the department store movement in this country in inevitably linked. In 1866 there was founded in New York City the firm of L. Straus and Sons, a wholesale business in crockery, glassware, and china. Although Mr. Straus possessed only $6,000 in capital at the start, he managed to sell ten times that amount in the first year of operation.

Several years before a Mr. Roland H. Macy had opened a small fancy store that carried a full line of dry goods and nothing else that was sold at less than regular prices. Macy steadily increased the amount of direct buying for his store and found it profitable to enter into a leased arrangement with the Straus'. A china and silverware department was added and it grew into the largest one in the store in terms of sales. By 1884 its merchandise was being displayed not only in the basement, but also on the street and second floors as well. The china department regularly quoted odd prices and subsequently this extended to other departments in the store. Here too was begun the mention of a bargain counter.

In 1887 the Straus' who were in continuous contact with Macy were admitted as partners. With their account of investments and joint partnership a new era in Macy's history began and department store retail trade has grown to its present size.

In 1893 the Straus' acquired Wetchler's and Abraham's from which ultimately grew Abraham and Straus, the leading department store in Brooklyn.

61.   THE FIRST GRAND OPERA PRODUCTIONS
IN ENGLISH IN AMERICA

For a long time the citizens of New York had been listening to opera. The Metropolitan Opera House had been offering opera year after year, but always at a loss.

In 1889 a young man who had made money in the cigar trade by the name of Oscar Hammerstein built a block of apartment houses in Harlem. Long a lover of music he had composed musical comedies, opera, and music for the ballet. In order to attract tenants, he thought it a good idea to build an opera house on his block. With this in mind in 1889, he erected a theater known as the Harlem Theater where for the first time in America he introduced the singing of operas in English. It proved to be a very great success and from then on he went on building theater after theater in the Times Square section of Broadway until he owned seven. The citizens of New York flocked to these large handsome buildings to see artists who could act as well as sing using the language that was familiar to them all.

The Metropolitan Opera Company was startled by his successes and purchased him outright at the price of $1,000,000. After the sale he continued to infuse his own personality in the companies policy and grand opera ever after was rendered exciting and popular.

Musical as well as scientific, Hammerstein is said to have taken out over ninety-six patterns for various inventions that were responsible for many improvements in the cigar trade. In addition to being the first to find a way of stripping tobacco, he also invented a way of applying air suction to the manufacture of cigars which brought him a fortune. As a result of these activities, cigar making became a factory process and forever put an end to the making of cigars in unhealthy basements. His "American Tobacco Journal" was considered the best in the trade.

In 1919 Hammerstein conceived the plan of having a municipal owned opera house in every large American community.

He offered to help build them if municipalities would operate them on the popularly devised Carnegie Library Plan. However, his plan was cut short by his death.

62. THE FIRST JEWISH MUSEUM IN AMERICA

The Semitic Museum, conducted under the auspices of Harvard University and located in Cambridge, Massachusetts, is America's first Jewish Museum. It was established in 1889 "to gather, preserve, and exhibit all the known kinds of material illustrating the life, history, and thought of the Semitic peoples and to increase the knowledge of the Semitic past in the explorations of Semitic countries and ruins."

The Museum Building is the gift of Jacob H. Schiff who gave $10,000 to the University, as are many of the objects in the Museum which illustrate the subjects of Semitic instruction.

From time to time, the Semitic Museum publishes the results of its investigations to show what have been the Semitic contributions to civilization. The Museum itself contains various objects dating back to the Egyptian and Roman periods in Jewish life such as glass bowls, jars, wine and oil jugs, lamps, arrowhead, wedding rings, amulets, and replicas of ancient tombstones. Here the sense of continuity in Jewish life takes on reality and one feels that a civilization of such breadth and such length has much yet to offer to human progress.

The Jewish Museum, conducted under the auspices of the Jewish Theological Seminary, and located in New York City, while it embodies these general purposes, at the same time has undertaken other functions. It is also a home of living Jewish art and contains the works of the greatest contemporary Jewish artists. In 1947 it acquired its present home, the fifty-four room home of the Felix Warburg's, the daughter and son-in-law of Jacob H. Schiff.

Among the exquisite collections the New York Museum contains the Torah Ark, brought by Solomon Schechter from the Cairo Synagogue in 1896. This Ark dates back to the thirteenth century and is the oldest piece of Jewish ecclesiastical furniture in the world. This Museum also contains by far, the largest collection of medals and plaques in the Western Hemisphere, over 1,000, the gifts of Samuel Friedenberg of New York City. These medallians of illustrious men and women in Jewish civilization, artistically and systematically arranged, demonstrate beyond any doubt that Jews and Judaism have always played an active and significant role in the development of human civilization.

63. THE FIRST READY MADE CLOTHING FOR CHILDREN

Children's clothing made by machine has become a permanent fixture in the American home and constitutes big business. Yet until comparatively recently, even while clothing manufacturers were developing the art of ready-made suits for men, and dresses and cloaks for women, little thought was given to do anything of the kind for children. It was still thought that every mother with a needle and thread could laboriously put together a garment good enough for children. The situation did not undergo any change until a poverty-stricken Jewish immigrant by the name of Louis Borgenicht, coming to America from a small Galician village and beginning as a peddler in the New York ghetto, saw his opportunity in 1889 and had the foresight to start a new American industry.

His story was at first the ordinary account of the poor alien struggling for a foothold amidst his new surrounding. Promoted to pushcart merchandising, he sold pots, pans, socks and stockings. Then he noticed that no one in the whole city of New York was making children's aprons. Without any capital, but with the aid of his wife, he began to make such aprons, which he peddled from house to house.

From the making of aprons he turned to the making of children's dresses. He came to the conclusion that ready-made clothes would save mothers endless work, the material and sewing would be better than home-made and the prices would be lower than that of similar mother-made garments.

Although when Borgenicht started there were three other New York manufacturers making children's dresses in a limited way, one an East Side tailor who sewed them to order, and two other enterprises that turned out expensive special garments, his creative energy by far made him the pioneering leader.

With a leap and a bound America became clothes conscious in those days of the ending decade of the century. Soon there were countless competitors. As Borgenicht kept ahead of the rest, he soon became known as the "King of the Children's Dress Trade," and his business grew into many millions. Ready-made children's clothing appeared from Maine to California. He had created a modern miracle business — an American industry designed to make American home life easier, more colorful and more democratic — and exceeding fifty million dollars a year.

64. THE FIRST CHIEF RABBI
OF AMERICAN ORTHODOX JEWRY

Rabbi Jacob Joseph, who in 1890 was appointed Chief Rabbi of American Orthodox Jewry, was the first and only Chief Rabbi it ever had.

Rabbi Joseph who was born in Kovne, Russia in 1848, studied at the world famous Yeshiva of Volozhin under Hirsch Leib Berlin and Israel Salanter. He was rabbi of several lesser Jewish communities, when in 1883 he was appointed maggid or preacher of the Jewish community of Vilna. In 1890 the orthodox Jewish Community of New York City summoned him to become their head, a position he retained until his death in 1902.

In 1900 he founded the Bes Sefer Yeshiva, which was destined to become the father of the Jewish parochial school movement which is now sweeping the country. After his death the name of the school was changed to the Rabbi Jacob Joseph Yeshiva. Today it is the largest Yeshiva in America and has close to a thousand students who combine their elementary school English studies together with Hebrew studies.

Rabbi Joseph gained considerable renown as a student of

Rabbi Jacob Joseph

the Talmud and was famous as a preacher. In 1888 he published "Lebeth Yaakov," a collection of his homilies and notes to rabbinic writings, of which a new Warsaw edition appeared in 1900.

His funeral was attended by 20,000 Jews. As the procession was passing by the factory of R. Hoe and Company, on the East Side of New York City, workmen and apprentices, began jeering and throwing bolts and nuts from the upper windows. This precipitated a riot in which many of the mourners were injured or mistreated by the police.

Rabbi Jacob Joseph's grandson, the former State Senator Lazarus Joseph, is presently Controller General of the City of New York. His son, the great-grandson and namesake of Rabbi Joseph, enlisted in the United States Marines in 1938 after graduating from Columbia University and became a Captain in the Solomon Islands, the scene of furious fighting, probably the youngest officer in that rank in the Marine Corps. He was killed in action in June, 1942, the very day his father was leaving his home for an appointment in Washington with Lt. General Thomas Holcomb, Commander of the United States Marine Corps, to discuss joining the service himself. A playground facing the Rabbi Jacob Joseph Yeshiva bears Captain Joseph's name.

65. THE FIRST YIDDISH THEATER IN AMERICA

America today has the best Yiddish Theaters in the world under the best directors, and much popular interest in the theater; but its first Yiddish Theater was not founded until 1890.

Throughout the latter part of the nineteenth century, the names of American Jews who produced plays and managed theaters are very prominent and would result in a fairly complete history of the American theater itself. David Belasco, a playright, actor, and director, produced four hundred plays and contributed many significant innovations to the Broadway theater (see Ch. 57). Charles Frohman, another great producer

who made his first production "Stranger in Paris" in 1883,
brought many leading personalities to the American stage. The
founder of the Yiddish Theater was Abraham Goldfaden, whose
opera, "Shulamith," is still often played. After him came Boris
Thomashefsky whose initial efforts in importing actors to America
suitable for the Yiddish stage at first came to naught.

With a small group of actors, mostly amateurs Thomashefsky
formed a troupe and began giving two performances a week.
The first theater was a small stage rented in the Old Bowery
Garden. Not very long afterwards, a far superior rival group of
actors arrived from London, and forced the former group to
disband. In 1890 with the arrival of Jacob Adler to this country, most victorious years followed. The Jews flocked to the new
theater to see one of the greatest actors of the day. For many
years Jacob Gordin, who wrote seventy plays, some originals
and some translations, was its principal writer. For some years
the Yiddish theater produced more vaudeville than drama, but
finally there came a revival.

In 1918 Maurice Schwartz and Ben Ami, two talented Yiddish
actors, leased the Irving Place Theater, a former playhouse,
and introduced art into the Yiddish theater. With "Dos Verfor-
fen Vinkel" they scored a great success and moved into the
Second Avenue Theater which once was the site of Peter Stuyvesant's estate. This Theater has since produced remarkable
original plays by excellent writers and the movement has spread
to other leading American cities.

For the most part, the Yiddish theater derived its main
strength from authors and musicians whose genius is rooted
in the phenomena of Jewish life. Its leading spirits have been:
Sholom Aleichem, who gave the theater, "Tevye," "Hard To Be
A Jew," "Wandering Stars," and "Stempenyu"; I. L. Peretz who
wrote "Der Golom," "Der Nier Nigun," and others; and I. J.
Singer, whose "Yoshe Kalb" is an extraordinary landscape of
movement and form, and who is responsible for those great
epic chronicles, "The Family Carnovsky" and "The Brothers
Ashkenazi." Its most famous composers are Achron, Chernyav-
sky, Olshenetsky and Rumshinsky.

One of the most significant decisions of the New York City

Opera Company was made in 1951 when the company decided to produce "The Dybuk," one of the most famous of all Yiddish plays during its forthcoming musical season, and which holds the highest box-office attendance at the Yiddish theaters throughout the country.

66.   THE FIRST PASTEURZED MILK STATIONS IN AMERICA

Jews have never felt that their charitable duties were discharged by providing for the needs of their fellow Jews. The Talmud goes beyond the Bible in its insistence on generosity. Always motivated by the humanitarian teachings of their religion, Jews have wholeheartedly born the philanthropic burden of the general community.

The story of pasteurized milk in this country begins with Nathan Straus, a member of the famous Straus family, whose gifts to humanity earned him the name of the "Greater Giver." (see Ch. 60). Fifty years ago the pasteurization of milk was not known. Thousands of babies died each year, but no one knew why. Straus began an investigation where infant mortality was the greatest. After visiting the slum districts of New York, he discovered that danger was present everywhere from the milk that people drank for no dairies were supervised and many of them were very dirty. Not long thereafter, Straus attended a convention of physicians and scientists in Brussels where Louis Pasteur, a French scientist, showed that milk could be purified of disease germs by heating. When Mr. Straus returned to America in 1892, he started a movement at once to pasteurize the milk (as it was called from Pasteur's name). His laboratory began distributing pasteurized milk very cheaply to poor people and in the hot summer months without charge for poor babies. In the first year alone over 34,000 bottles were given out. As a result of Straus' activities the lives of thousands of babies were saved and the terrible death rate was cut in half. Within twenty years milk inspection became a part of the state administration everywhere; much milk was pasteurized, and the children of the nation benefited. Mr. Straus alone was responsible for this great humanitarian work. He saved thousands of lives and spared many others from illness.

But that was not all. During the sad winter following the panic of 1892 he distributed over a million and a half baskets of coal for five cents each to the New York poor. The next year he distributed over a million tickets for fuel, lodging, and food. His benefactions made him one of the great helpers of his own people and the American people as a whole. In 1923 the people of New York acclaimed him their greatest benefactor in the field of social welfare. President Taft said of him: "Nathan Straus is a great Jew and the greatest Christian of us all."

67.   THE FIRST VISITING NURSES

Fifty-eight years ago, a frightened, tearful child stood in the doorway of a tenement room on New York's Lower East Side and sobbed to the nurse inside who was conducting a class on home care of the sick, "My mamma's sick. Please won't you come home with me?"

Instantly, the nurse dismissed the class and hurried with the child to where the sick mother lay.

Lillian D. Wald, trained nurse, opened a new chapter in humanitarian service when she answered that little girl's call. Stemming from the famous Henry Street settlement which she founded and which became the "heart" of her activities, this chapter is filled with stories of improved health conditions, cleaner, safer homes, and the saving of many lives.

Miss Wald was born in Rochester, N. Y. in 1867 and moved from there with her family to Ohio when she was quite young. Here she was reared in luxury, but instead of the social life she might have had, she chose to take a nurse's training course at the New York hospital and to dedicate herself to the service of others.

After her graduation, she began to hold classes to teach people how to care for sickness in the home. She had seen through her kind, sympathetic eyes, how frightened people were by sickness and how it made them helpless. Together with her friend Mary Brewster, who was also a nurse, she went to live in the tenement district of New York's Lower East Side where the people needed her help the most and began a nurses' service. Thus began the first visiting nurses in the world. Little did she realize that less than fifty years later there would be an army of more than twenty thousand visiting nurses in the United States.

Soon after her nursing service began, Miss Wald saw that her quarters were not nearly large enough to care for the throngs who came for her help. Therefore, she moved to Henry Street, to the settlement that became so important that one little boy said he thought that "God must live there."

When Miss Wald saw the noisy and littered streets which served as the only playground the East Side children knew, she turned the backyard of the settlement into a little park where children and grownups might play and rest in the fresh air and sunlight. Thanks to the fine example set by her, city playgrounds have been established all over the United States.

In 1902 Miss Wald organized the first city school nursing work in the world and America became the first country to start a regular medical care for school children. She also started the first "bedside school" for handicapped children which was the pattern for many such schools now found in many parts of the country.

Sickness and tragedy received another blow when she told the authorities to organize a Federal Children's Bureau which was established by Congress in 1908.

68.   THE FIRST UNIFORMS FOR WOMEN

The history of the Jew in nineteenth century America is marked by his development of the clothing industry. Starting in the eighteen-thirties, with factories that produced crude, cheaply made clothing, he developed the industry so well that by the end of the century, dresses for women and suits for men, of good quality and cut, were being produced in such qualities that their price was within the reach of most people; in this he helped to democratize American society.

Into this picture fits Henry A. Dix, who came to America in 1892 from a small, poverty-stricken village in the Ukraine, and had the foresight to start a new branch in women's wear — the manufacture of uniforms.

Soon after his arrival in America, Dix and his wife, attracted by the cheerful little village of Millville, New Jersey, decided to capitalize on their experience as shopkeepers in Russia by opening a dry goods store there. They supplemented their shop-keeping by peddling through the country-side, selling the rural population "Mother Hubbard" wrappers for everyday wear and "tea gowns" of flowered sateens for Sunday wear that had been produced in the New York sweatshops. One day they came to the conclusion that if they themselves could produce something that was better-looking and cost no more, women would prefer to buy such garments.

With no knowledge of manufacturing, and with no acquaintance with dressmaking or tailoring, husband and wife designed and made their first gowns. Then they found a youth who had worked in a Philadelphia dressmaking shop and hired him for twelve dollars a week as mechanic and designer. The village girls were hired as operators. Their garments grew steadily better and before long they were turning out something which was far ahead of anything else at the price on the market.

From the very first, Dix insisted that every garment should be marked "made by Henry A. Dix" and that it should be simple in style, of good material and carefully stitched. In competition with "job lot" cheap wrappers and house dresses, he emphasized quality — "not how cheap, but how good" his merchandise could be for the price.

In 1896 came a development in his business — a switch to the making of uniforms for working girls, so that help in hotels, waitresses in restaurants, maids in a household and saleswomen in shops might have available simple, neat costumes. Up to that time the working girl, while on her job, had made use of any old second-best dress.

The same Dix standard of quality, taste, workmanship, simplicity and fair prices applied to the "Dix Uniforms." They became a popular success from coast to coast. Thus a new branch of the women's wear industry was created.

In 1917 during World War I when the Red Cross adopted a nurse's hospital uniform, it turned to Dix to design it (see Ch. 55). Then the Dix Red Cross uniform took its place as international insignia and became recognized in whatever corner of the earth suffering called for the ministering of that noble institution. Soon thereafter the United States Government appointed Dix to supply army and navy nurses' uniforms.

In 1922, looking back over his seventy-two years, long years of struggle with never an idle day, Henry Dix essentially a man of simple tastes now grown rich, faced the problem of the future. As the year grew to a close, he turned his business over to his employees. To satisfy public curiosity of his gift, newspapers blazed forth with the first incident of its kind in American history:

"Man Who Gave Worker $1,000,000 Business Calls It Merely Justice . . . Dix never had a strike in a quarter of a century. Has made all he wants — declined big price for plant so his employees could have a chance"

The Dix story ends in 1938, the year in which he died at the age of eighty-eight; but after him lives the institution he founded and his ideals so typically American.

69. THE FIRST HEBREW LETTER
ISSUED BY THE AMERICAN GOVERNMENT

The first Hebrew letter ever issued by the United States Government was sent by Secretary of State John Hay in 1902 to Rabbi Marcus Dubov of Evansville, Indiana.

Rabbi Marcus had written earlier to express his gratitude to Secretary Hay for his efforts on behalf of Rumanian Jewry. The Hebrew letter signed by Secretary Hay was prepared by a Mr. Thomas, official translator of the State Department, who knew Hebrew well. This is the only time that Hebrew was used in an official document of the United States Government.

The letter in English translation reads as follows:

"Man of God: I received the letter and I was glad that my work for the persecuted brethren in the kingdom of Roumania found favor in thy sight. Peace be to thee and to the Congregation B'nai Moshe.

I pray that the Lord our God may bless all of thy brethren in Evansville in all their efforts, physically and spiritually, and that the God of Peace may be with thee forever. I will remain thy friend,

John Hay"

The first time that Hebrew was officially used in international diplomacy was when Aubrey Eban, youngest delegate at the United Nations, representing Israel, the youngest state on earth, signed the genocide convention in the language of the Bible.

70. THE FIRST JEWISH WOMAN SUPERINTENDENT OF SCHOOLS IN AMERICA

Women now hold so many offices in public life that it is a little strange to remember that the first woman and the first Jewish district superintendent of schools in a great American city was appointed no longer ago than in 1903.

This distinction was bestowed upon Julia Richman who was born in New York in 1855 six years before the outbreak of the Civil War. Julia was a clever girl and learned quickly. She was educated at Hunter College and New York University. When she was seventeen years of age, she began to teach in a grammar school in the city and proved herself to be a very successful teacher. From the year 1872 to the time of her death in 1912 she introduced many thorough methods of teaching and the New York Public School System was to undergo a series of reforms such as it had never seen before. Her ideas gained ground and she won the approval of the leading educators of the day who supported her with their influence.

Miss Richman developed methods of progressive pedagogy, established the first Parent Teachers' Association and made arrangements for the correction of defective vision in school children. It was largely due to her efforts that classes for defective children became part of the New York educational system, and she organized one of the first classes. It was through her influence that eye examinations were conducted in schools as part of the regular classroom procedure. She also established an agency for children who were forced to leave school and seek employment.

In 1903 when she rose to be District Superintendent of Schools, she was given the privilege of selecting the district she wanted. She chose New York's Lower East Side and left her uptown home to reside among the people to whose uplift she devoted her life work.

The Julia Richman High School, one of the largest in New York and the first high school in America to bear the name of a Jewish woman, was named in her memory to commemorate her contribution to the public school system.

71. THE FIRST AMERICAN JEWISH INTERNATIONAL FINANCIER

Jacob Henry Schiff, the most beloved American Jewish philanthropist of his generation and internationally respected financier of the 1900's, lived at the time when America was becoming a great industrial power. It was the gay period of Diamond Jim Brady and Lillian Russell. It was the era of the railroads, growing factories and expansion.

Schiff came from a distinguished and scholarly family of rabbis and business men in Frankfort on the Main, Germany, where he was born in 1847. At the age of eighteen, he left for America, and ten years later was admitted as a member of the firm of Kuhn, Loeb and Company, private bankers. He displayed such financial skill that in 1885, he replaced Loeb, his father-in-law upon his retirement. In his capacity as head of the firm, he loaned hundreds of millions of dollars to business enterprises, trust companies and railroad builders such as Harriman and Hill who opened up the empire of the west to settlement. Through the successes of these enterprises, he and his firm became immensely wealthy, until they were the second largest private banking firm in America.

In 1905 during the Russo-Japanese War, his firm loaned huge sums of money to Japan. For the floating of the bond issue of $200,000,000 for the Japanese government, the most outstanding achievement in international finance since the inception of America, he was awarded the highest Japanese decoration ever given to an American.

Such an immensely wealthy and successful business man could help Jewish causes on an unprecedented scale if he wished, and he did. During the vicious Russian pogroms of 1903-5, Schiff helped organize a committee to raise the unprecedented sum of $1,750,000 for the relief of the victims of the massacres. The following year he sponsored the American Jewish Committee and was active in its work until the time of his death.

Schiff was himself educated in Hebrew and Jewish learning, so that he was equally interested in the promotion of Jewish learning. A roll call of the Jewish educational activities and insituations that owe their existence or at least their establishment on a sound foundation would include most of the major undertakings in the sphere of Jewish scholarship; the Teachers' Institute of the Jewish Theological Seminary and of the Hebrew Union College, the Jewish Encyclopedia, the Hebrew Press of the Jewish Publication Society, the Semitic Museum at Harvard, the Jewish Book and Manuscript Collection at the Jewish Theological Seminary, the Library of Congress and the New York Public Library.

In creating these landmarks of Jewish learning, Schiff was guided not only by personal reverence for the traditions and culture of the Jewish people, but a deep desire to find a means of revitalizing that culture. It was this motivation that prompted him at the very beginning of his career as a patron of Jewish learning to come to the support of agencies dedicated to educating Jewish youth to an awakening of an awareness and appreciation for the traditions and cultural treasures towards whose perpetuation he did so much. (see Ch. 52).

Schiff was interested in the cultural and economic develop-

Jacob Henry Schiff

ment of Palestine and gave one hundred thousand dollars for the founding of the Haifa Technicum. But he was never content to let his money work for him. In the Montifiore Home in New York, of which he was president, he used to spend many hours talking to the patients, eating their regular fare with them, not only helping them from the outside, but trying to see the world from the angle of their poverty and their misery.

It was the blending of statesmanship and of a statesman's vision with the urgency of his heart that rendered Schiff incomparable among the philanthropists of his period. Although a good deal of his far flung philanthropy was anonymous, none of his gifts went out carelessly. He sat on the boards of many institutions, continually made inquires about the welfare of those concerned, and talked with their workers.

A few weeks before his death, Schiff corresponded on the subject of a loan for Palestine with Sir Herbert Samuel, the High Commissioner. He believed that it was possible to finance a Palestine project then underway and that the country would be rebuilt in accordance with the terms of the Balfour Declaration. His death unfortunately put an end to this work.

He died September 25, 1920.

72.   THE FIRST JEWISH CABINET MEMBER IN AMERICA

American Jews had achieved fame as public servants and gained a great deal of respect for their ability. They had occupied almost every office in the land, not always in proportion to their numbers, but certainly enough to prove their patriotism and loyalty.

In 1906 President Theodore Roosevelt chose Oscar S. Straus, after whom a memorial is being dedicated in Washington, D. C., to serve in the newly created Department of Commerce and Labor. Now for the first time in American history, a Jew occupied a cabinet post.

Member of the distinguished Straus family and a son of Lazarus Straus, one of the founders of R. H. Macy and Company, Oscar Straus studied law at Columbia University Law

The Hon. Oscar S. Straus

113

School (see Ch. 60). At the age of twenty-three he entered into private practice. He became interested in politics and took part in New York public affairs. From that time on the career of Oscar Straus was rapid and brilliant in law practice and business, in scholarship, authorship, and finally in public service.

His devotion to his country led Straus to make a special study of its institutions and the men who laid the foundations of the republic. This resulted in the concrete expression of two notable books which attracted general attention. The first of these, "The Origin of the Republican Form of Government," was the first attempt of its kind, to trace with skill and scholarship the rise of American democracy from the Hebrew Commonwealth as expounded in the Bible. The second, entitled, "Roger Williams, Pioneer of Religious Liberty in the United States," earned for him the honorary degree of L.H.D. from Brown University.

President Grover Cleveland was greatly impressed by these unusual publications and appointed Straus three times to serve as United States Ambassador to Turkey. Straus accepted the position although he was not the first Jew to hold a high diplomatic post, for beginning with the appointment by President Monroe of Mordecai Manuel Noah as consul to Tunis there had been more than twenty Jews in the diplomatic service of the United States.

The public work of Oscar Straus led him from the service of the nation to the cause of world peace and the service of all nations. Upon his return from Turkey he was appointed as one of the four American representatives to the Court of Arbitration at the Hague, a position held for twenty-five years.

As a loyal Jew, Straus was one of the founders and the first president of the American Jewish Historical Society. This was not his only Jewish activity. As early as 1874, he had been a leader in the formation of the YMHA in New York. He was a trustee of the Jewish Publication Society in Philadelphia, and a member of the executive committee of the American Jewish Committee, a governor of Dropsie College and a director of the Hebrew Orphan Asylum in New York.

Above all he was a leader in all activities in behalf of the unfortunate Russian Jews who were the victims of pogroms during the closing years of the nineteenth century and the early years of the twentieth.

He died on May 3, 1926.

The second American Jew to hold a cabinet position was Henry Morgenthau, Jr., the son of a universally prominent man who had served as United States Ambassador to Turkey. In 1934 President Franklin D. Roosevelt appointed him Secretary of the Treasury. Thus at the age of forty-two, Morgenthau was one of the youngest men to hold the second highest ranking position in the cabinet, a position he retained for twelve years.

One of Morgenthau's first major undertakings was the sale of United States Savings bonds to the public which later as war bonds became an auxiliary means of financing expenditures during World War II. At the end of the war, the United Jewish Appeal which was organized for refugee oversea needs, called upon him to become their first general chairman and head its campaign to save the remnant of European Jewry.

Today Morgenthau heads the American Financial and Development Corporation for Israel and is chairman of the Board of Governors of the State of Israel's $500,000,000 bond issue drive.

73. THE FIRST FREE SYNAGOGUE IN AMERICA

Rabbi Stephen Samuel Wise, one of the key leaders of American Jewry for a period of over fifty-five years, was born in Budapest of a distinguished family of rabbis. He was brought to the United States at the age of one and as a youth was slated to be a rabbi. He received his rabbinical training privately and in 1901 completed his studies for the P.H.D. degree at Columbia University.

In 1893, young Wise took his first position as Assistant Rabbi of the Madison Avenue Synagogue of New York. Seven years later he was called to Portland, Oregon where he officiated until 1906. Early in that year he was invited to discuss a call to the pulpit of Temple Emanuel in New York City. A dispute over the freedom of the pulpit arose between him and Louis Marshall, its president. Rabbi Wise thereupon renounced the proposed

Rabbi Stephen S. Wise

116

post and in 1907 founded in New York City the Free Synagogue which under his influence became one of the most influential congregations in the country.

Rabbi Wise breathed the air of freedom and he wanted freedom for all the underprivileged of the earth. He wanted that freedom for the American people. He demanded that freedom for the Jewish people. Gifted with oratorical powers, Rabbi Wise became the voice of America's millions. Because of the lack of space in his own quarters, he was soon obliged to hold Sunday services in Carnegie Hall which was frequently filled to capacity.

Whether in the struggle for trade unionism, for greater democracy in politics, for civil liberties, or for the protection of American democracy among the nations of the earth, Rabbi Wise thundered against tyranny and oppression, against Fascism and dictatorship. A friend of presidents and of simple folk, a lover of humanity, and a doer of small and great deeds, he emerged from the Free Synagogue to become America's statesman without portfolio. Thousands learned the meaning of the word "democracy" through the example of the life of Rabbi Wise. In carrying the burden of the two great bodies he helped to create — the Zionist Organization of America and the American Jewish Congress, he was constantly considered spokesman for the "little Jew."

To perpetuate his ideals in 1922, he founded in New York City, the Jewish Institute of Religion, where young Jews could be trained for leadership in the rabbinate, education and social service (see Ch. 48).

He died in 1949, loyal to his Jewish heritage as he had lived, and dedicated to the service of his people and his country.

74. THE FIRST JEWISH NOBEL PRIZE WINNER

Alfred Bernhard Nobel, the Swedish engineer, philanthropist and educator, established five prizes of $42,280 each to be awarded annually for the most important discoveries in physics, in chemistry, in physiology and medicine; also for the best effort to promote peace during the year and for the most distinguished work of literature. Jews have taken ten percent of all Nobel prizes. In 1907 Professor Albert A. Michelson, professor of physics at the University of Chicago, was the first American and the first Jew to receive the Nobel Prize.

Professor Michelson, who was German born, came to this country while still very young. He began his teaching career in the field of physics and chemistry upon his graduation from the United States Naval Academy at Annapolis. There he began to conduct his epoch making light-measurement experiments. After many years of research he made one of the greatest scientific discoveries of the age by computing that light travels 186,213 miles per second, paving the way for one of the most startling of modern conceptions, Einstein's theory of relativity.

By devising the instrument known as the inferometer, Professor Michaelson made it possible for scientists for the first time to measure the diameter of the stars. This marvelous instrument with its exactitude in measuring the tiniest quantities of space and matter could make discoveries of great importance. Our knowledge of radioactivity, vitamins, hormones and their activity in the human body, was all made possible by the use of this instrument.

The first "Distinguished Professorship" ever awarded by the University of Chicago was awarded to Michelson in recognition of his remarkable record as an original discoverer in the field of physics. In addition to the honorary degrees from a large number of universities, membership in scientific societies in this country and abroad, a number of national and international awards, he has received every honor which can be given to a scientist, of which the Nobel Prize is the best known.

75. THE FIRST AMERICAN PORTRAIT COIN

The first coin bearing the head of a president of the United States, the Lincoln penny, issued by the Treasury Department on August 2, 1909, was designed by a Jewish artist, Victor David Brenner, whose initials, VDB appeared on the first

28,000,000 of these coins. This was the first potrait coin ever used in American currency.

Brenner was born in Lithuania in 1871 and came to the United States in 1890. As a young boy he first obtained employment as a die cutter and engraver of badges in an Essex Street shop in Lower New York City. At night he attended art classes at Cooper Union and later at the National Academy of Design and Art. In 1893 he set himself up in business as a die cutter and engraver for jewelers and silversmiths, prospered, and sent for his family.

One day while Professor Ettinger, a well-known coin collector of the City College of the City of New York was browsing around the East Side, he entered Brenner's shop and was attracted by a head of Beethoven which Brenner had done for a musical society. His interest in the young immigrant brought about an introduction to the Numismatic Society through which Brenner won the commission to design a medal which brought him into prominence. He was enabled to study at Paris under Louis Oscar Rotz, ranking medalist of Europe and Alexandre Charpentier, member of the Rodin group. Under these new influences Brenner's work developed in scope, and in recognition of his work, he won a bronze medal at a Paris exhibition and several other awards at American cities. After extensive travels throughout Europe, Brenner came home to throw himself at once into the battle being waged by the Numismatic Society for better American coins. The movement met with hearty approval from President Theodore Roosevelt, whose head was being modeled by Brenner for the obverse side of the Panama Medal which is awarded to every workman who puts in two years of labor on the canal. During one of the sitting sessions, Brenner showed Roosevelt a design of a Lincoln plaque which so impressed the president that he urged the Treasury Department to adopt it as a first step in reforming the face of the United States coinage. But to Brenner, this was more than just a chance commission. He expressed the desire that the design be used on a one cent piece, in order that it have the widest circulation possible, and thus familiarize even the most humble with President Lincoln's face.

In 1910 Brenner wrote "The Art of the Medal," a leading book in the field. He achieved further prominence with his bust of Charles Eliot Norton which is in the Fogg Museum at Harvard. His famous bas-relief of Washington may be seen today in the Federal Building in Pittsburgh, and his bas-relief of Lincoln in the Washington Irving High School in New York.

76. THE FIRST MOVING PICTURE

Ever since 1894 when the Holland brothers opened up the first penny arcade peep show on Herald Square, the citizens of New York could not stay away from the knickelodeons. The pictures they saw were only a few minutes long — "Bronco Billy" chasing a train and falling on his face, children throwing pillows at each other, or a couple of drunks running away from each other.

In 1896 a fourteen year old boy who was born in the Jewish section of Warsaw, Poland came to the United States. Little did Samuel Goldfish, as he was then called, realize that he was destined to become its first and foremost motion-picture producer. During his early years in New York, he became a glove salesman and then chief sales executive for a glove company at the then fabulous salary of close to $15,000 a year. But he too was drawn into the moviemania of the time and frequented the knickelodeons. But Sam was completely enthralled. He would come home and pester his brother-in-law, Jesse Lasky, to go into the picture business. He had an idea that full-length stories and plays could be made into moving pictures.

By 1913 Goldfish had left a successful career as a glove salesman to help produce the first feature-length moving picture ever made in Hollywood — an epic of American Indians and London high society called "The Squaw Man." The picture was made in a rented stable near the present intersection of Sunset Boulevard and Vine Street. At night coyotes came down from the hills to prowl around the building. Cecile B. DeMille, the director shot a couple of them and nailed their skins to the wall.

DeMille was one of Goldfish's partners in this pioneer enterprise. So was Lasky, who started as a cornet player and became one of the best-known vaudeville and cabaret impressarios in America. Arthur S. Friend, a theatrical lawyer, was the fourth member of the group. Each of these men invested $5,000 in an organization known as the Jesse Lasky Feature Play Company. Another $5,000 in stock was set aside for general sale, while $5,000 more went to Dustin Farnum as salary for playing the lead in "The Squaw Man." At the last moment, Farnum who was offered his salary in stocks backed out and demanded his $5,000 in cash. He got his money, but three years later the stock he refused was worth more than a million dollars.

DeMille and Lasky kept their stock and eventually became multimillionaires, and they are now prominent producers and leading figures in the Hollywood motion-picture industry.

In 1916 the production joined with Edgar and Arch Selwyn and the new organization was called the Goldwyn Pictures Corporation, a name manufactured from the first syllable of Goldfish and the last syllable of Selwyn.

The more Goldfish saw and heard the name Goldwyn, the more he liked it and annexed it for his personal use.

Goldwyn has been producing moving-pictures longer than any other producer in the world. He has made such fine and interesting films as: "Street Scene," "Arrowsmith," Dead End," "Wuthering Heights," "Dodsworth," "The Dark Angel," "The Little Foxes," "Stella Dallas," and "The Best Years of Our Lives." The latter produced in 1946 was acclaimed the best picture of the year and received an unprecedented total of nine awards.

Other Jews brought to the industry the talents so essential for theatrical undertakings; producers like Louis B. Mayer, and the Warner Brothers; and stars like Al Jolson, Eddie Cantor, Paul Muni and Edward G. Robinson.

Today the motion picture industry brings entertainment to eighty-five million people weekly. It provides employment for hundreds of thousands of persons, and plays an increasingly important role in molding our social and cultural ideals.

77. THE FIRST JEWISH GOVERNOR IN AMERICA

Many American Jews have taken part in municipal, state, and national affairs. Some of them have risen to high public office.

Four western states, which have very few Jews, have elected Jews as governors in recent years.

The first Jew to hold this position was Moses Alexander, who was governor of Idaho for two terms, from 1915 to 1919.

Alexander's family had emigrated to the United States in 1868 and had settled in Chillicothe, Missouri. He left school while quite young and obtained a position as a clerk in a clothing store. A few years later, he owned the store. He became interested in local politics and in 1886, served on the city council of Chillicothe. In view of his splendid record, he was elected mayor, and saved the town from bankruptcy. In 1891 because of ill health, he was forced to leave Missouri, and went to Boise, Idaho. Here, he opened a clothing store, which soon developed into a thriving chain-store business. Alexander entered the political field again and was elected mayor for one term, from 1897 to 1899, and then reelected again in 1901. In the fall of 1914, after having proven himself a devoted public servant of his state and country, he was elected governor of Idaho, and served for two terms.

In the election of Moses Alexander as governor, a precedent was established. He was chosen to the foremost office in the state without seeking or expectation and guided the destinies of his state on the convictions of his neighbors. Simon Bamberger, a Jewish merchant of Salt Lake City, was elected governor of Utah shortly afterwards. He was the first Democrat and the first non-Mormon to become Governor.

When President Franklin D. Roosevelt took office in 1933, there were four Jewish governors in the United States. They were: Governor Herbert Lehman of New York, Governor Henry Horner of Illinois, Governor Julius Meir of Oregon and Governor Arthur Seligman of New Mexico.

After having served as Governor of New York for four terms, in 1949, Herbert Lehman was elected to the United States Senate from New York, and thus achieved the distinction of being the first Jew to be elected to the Senate by popular vote. Other American Jews who served in the Senate had been appointed or elected by the several state legislatures before the enactment of the Seventeenth Amendment which called for the election to the Senate by popular vote.

78.   THE FIRST UNITED STATES SUPREME COURT JUSTICE

Both in private practice and on the bench, American Jews have risen to high eminence in the profession of law.

Louis Dembitz Brandeis, who was described by President Wilson as "friend of justice and friend of man," was the first Jew to occupy the position of United States Supreme Court Justice.

Brandeis was born in Louisville, Kentucky, in 1856, to a young immigrant couple who had rebelled against their native Austria's lack of equal opportunity and left their fatherland to find freedom in America. His uncle, after whom he was named, was a member of the national convention that nominated Lincoln for president, and well-known as a scholar and writer on Jewish topics. As a young man Brandeis studied law at Harvard University. Upon graduation he formed a partnership with Samuel Warren and fixed up the first really modern law office that Boston had ever had. Within a short period of eight years he became the leading barrister of that city. By representing liberal causes before the courts and "little men" against great corporations, he became known as the "People's Lawyer." He worked out such splendid projects as the Massachusetts system of savings bank insurance and pensions for wage earners. In 1910 he was asked to act as arbitrator in the New York garment workers' strike, the largest New York had ever seen. In this capacity he originated constitutionalism in disputes between employer and employee.

Here for the first time Mr. Brandeis became interested in Jewish problems and was led to an intense study of Zionism. The idealist in him warmed to the thought of making Palestine once again the homeland of the Jewish people, and he became

Justice Louis D. Brandeis

124

a leader in the fight to reawaken the Jewish spirit and safeguard Jewish rights. In his uniquely terse and powerful style, he set down a credo that has become classic: "Loyalty to America demands that every Jew should be a Zionist." In 1916 when President Wilson appointed Mr. Brandeis to the Supreme Court, he was president of the Zionist Organization. (see Ch. 59).

Although the President at first was assailed for naming Brandeis to the highest court in the land, after a few years, Brandeis was hailed as America's greatest jurist and among the greatest lovers of justice the world has ever known. After a great career in both Jewish and American life, he died at the age of eighty-five.

In Israel a colony was established which proudly bears the name of Kfar Brandeis after the late justice whom the Jews of America were delighted to honor. In Waltham, Massachusetts, in 1948, another tribute was paid to his memory by naming a university after him.

Today, Brandeis University, the first Jewish sponsored institution of higher learning in this country which welcomes students of all races and religions, takes its place as a preeminent member of the American family of universities.

The second Jew to be appointed to the Supreme Court was Benjamin Nathan Cardozo, descended from a Spanish family which settled in America in the seventeenth century. His father was the first Jew to become justice of the Supreme Court of the State of New York. Justice Benjamin Cardozo's decisions were notable both for literary beauty and constitutional insight.

79. THE FIRST AMERICAN JEW TO RECEIVE THE MEDAL OF RECONNAISSANCE FRANCAISE

In 1917 the United States was again at war, this time against a ruthless foreign enemy who had sunk its ships, plotted its downfall and given every indication that it was bent on a course of conquest to embrace the entire world. Americans loved their country and were glad to defend the ideals which had inspired its growth. These ideals had a special meaning for Jews. When they saw the promise of America suddenly transmitted into a campaign to make it possible for these ideals to be extended and enjoyed by many more, the American Jew knew that it was his fight too.

From every nook and cranny of the nation over 140,000 Jews came in the service of the nation. From obscure ranches in the West all the way to the teeming tenements of New York, which sent thousands of Jews to the famous Seventy-Seventh Division, they came flocking to the colors. Their citations and awards for bravery were many. The story of Benjamin Kaufman who for many years was National Commander of the Jewish War Veterans of the United States is just one piece. For heroism in the field of battle nine governments heaped awards upon him and his own country gave him the Congressional Medal of Honor.

Enshrined in the history of the war's heroic exploits is the story of Clarence Baer who was the first American to receive the Medal of Reconnaissance Francaise from the French government, for exceptionally meritorious service in a duty of great responsibility.

80.   THE FIRST JEWISH
RADIO STATION MANAGER IN AMERICA

David Sarnoff, who became commercial manager of the newly, formed Radio Corporation of America in 1919, is one of radio's earliest pioneers. Ever advancing, he subsequently became general manager in 1921, vice-president in 1922, executive vice-president in 1929 and president in 1930, a position he now holds in addition to being chairman of the board of the National Broadcasting System.

There is no better example of the American way to success than the story of this great radio pioneer. David was born in Russia in 1891 and was brought to this country at the age of nine. He attended public school and later took a few courses in engineering. His interest in the telegraph led him to buy technical books on the subject which he studied at night. He actually began his career as personal message boy to Marconi when he came to this country. Before long he became a junior telegraph operator and in 1908 operator at the Marconi station at Siaconset, Nantucket Isle and within a year he went to sea on the S. S. Beathic headed for the Arctic. In telegraphing communications with an operator at Belle Isle, Labrador, he learned that the operator was very sick and took his symptoms He at once communicated with his ship's doctor who prescribed via telegraph, thus initiating the Marine Medical Service. David continued at sea the next few years, returning to become operator of the telegraph station at John Wanamaker's New York store.

On the night of April 14, 1912, the most thrilling night in his life occurred when Sarnoff picked up the tragic flash via wireless that the Titanic struck an iceberg and was sinking fast. For the next seventy-two hours all other stations were called off the air, Sarnoff directed the rescue and the whole nation became aware of the horror of the tragedy.

Throughout the next ten years he devoted himself entirely to radio and its improvement. In recognition to his numerous contributions to the field, at the age of thirty-one, he was made head of the most powerful radio organization in the world. As director and chairman of the board of the National Broadcasting Company, he was largely responsible for the improvement in the quality of radio programs. During World War II he served as a member of the United States Defense Communications Board and was appointed a Brigadier General under Eisenhower. Today he has branched out in television and is one of the world's most powerful figures in radio.

81. THE FIRST PIANO CONCERTO CREATED IN JAZZ

American Jews have shown unusual aptitude for the theater and for music. One of the first to be drawn into the new stream of popular music was a young Jewish boy by the name of George Gershwin. Gershwin was to prove himself one of the most brilliantly creative musical geniuses that America has yet produced.

It was by pure accident that Gershwin, who stemmed from a

family that was lacking in musical talent, became a song mill who converted his own vitality and love of life into a series of carefully written manuscripts, all jazz, the only music he ever wanted to write.

With the purchase of a piano that was bought more for decoration in his New York East Side apartment, than with the thought of having it played, he mastered all the knowledge that his twenty-five cents a lesson teacher could impart. Before long he began writing his own compositions and left school to devote himself entirely to a musical career. For a while, he plugged at songs in Tin Pan Alley, the Broadway section of New York, where popular songs are born. He always insisted that "jazz is American folk music" and was to prove to the world that popular songs could be planned as carefully as more formal compositions and could be as musically artistic.

Following the success of his first Broadway musical production "La Lucille" and the "George White Scandals," he was asked by Paul Whiteman, leader of the country's finest dance orchestra, to write a composition with a piano part to be played by the him, accompanied by the Whiteman band. Thus came to be written "Rhapsody in Blue," the emotional melody with the variety of moods which was forever to dispell prejudice against the use of jazz in symphonic music.

In 1925 Gershwin continued to make musical history when he was commissioned by Walter Damrosch, conductor of the New York Symphony Orchestra to write a concerto in which the piano played the solo part accompanied by the orchestra. This major composition, the first piano concerto ever created in jazz — Gershwin's so-called "Concerto in F" was orchestrated by Gershwin himself and presented for the first time in Carnegie Hall on December 3, 1925, with the composer playing the piano part. For thirty minutes Gershwin poured forth music full of enchanting tone subleties with a sincerity which won an ovation from the audience.

By the time Gershwin was thirty he had become internationally famous, and a nation hummed and whistled his songs. Before his early death, he had already composed the music for "An American in Paris," "Porgy and Bess" and "Of Thee I Sing" which was the first musical comedy to be published in book form and to receive the Pulitizer Prize for the best play of the year.

In 1930 a few years after Gershwin's death, the great English conductor, Albert Coates, listed the fifty best musical works of the generation. Only one American composition was included and but one American composer — George Gershwin and his "Concerto in F."

Today all Gershwin musical programs are annual features of the Stadium concerts given by the Philharmonic Symphony Orchestra in New York and millions of theaters, concert halls, and homes constantly play his rich and colorful melodies.

82.   THE FIRST STAR OF "TALKIES"

Alike on the stage, screen and radio, American Jewish artists are known and loved as entertainers. The first stars of "talkies" was a Jew by the name of Al Jolson.

Al Jolson, who was born Asa Yoelson in 1886 in Russia, was brought to this country at the age of seven. As a youngster struck with the lure of the stage lights, he travelled with vaudeville and minstrel shows, sang in cafes and saloons, and followed circuses. He made his first stage appearance in 1899 at the Herald Square Theater in New York, as one of the mob in Israel Zangwill's production "Children of the Ghetto." After a long period in vaudeville, he achieved major stardom in a musical comedy series of productions known as the "Winter Garden Shows" in which he was often referred to as "Gus" the blackface stock character.

At about this time the Warner Brothers, a family of Jewish immigrants who had established themselves as producers and distributors of motion pictures of the early knickolodian type, were the first to sense the possibilities of the use of sound as applied to motion pictures. After witnessing the demonstration of a new device, they acquired the vitaphone and produced the first full-length sound picture, the historic "Jazz Singer." Jolson was in the starring role and caused a revolt in the motion picture industry. Before the showing of this picture "talkies" were only an experiment. After its release they were put on a sound basis. Bringing to the industry the talents so essential for theatrical undertakings, Jolson also starred in "The Singing Fool" and "Mammy," the next two "talkies" that were made.

In 1932 after several other stage successes Jolson began his radio career as star of the first program in which running monologue was interspersed with songs.

With "The Jolson Story" (1947) and "Jolson Sings Again" (1949), two great Hollywood successes, Jolson skyrocketed to even greater heights.

When Jolson sang, something happened to audiences. He had a spirit, a quality that brought him close to every person that saw and heard him. Audiences felt what he saw. When he was sentimental, audiences wept — and frequently Jolson cried himself. When he shot onto a stage bursting with vitality and happiness, audiences grew suddenly happier. It was that quality that made him probably the most popular and most successful entertainer in American history.

Jolson died in November, 1950 in San Francisco. He had just returned from Korea, where he had given performances for soldiers. Twenty thousand persons jammed Hollywood Boulevard for his funeral. President Harry S. Truman sent a message that began:

"We have lost our Al."

Jolson wrote a will in which he left nine tenths of a $4,000,000 estate to charity. The money to be divided among Jewish, Catholic and Protestant causes.

83.   THE FIRST LIBERAL ARTS COLLEGE
UNDER JEWISH AUSPICES

Yeshiva College, the first college of liberal arts and sciences under Jewish auspices in the entire history of the Diaspora, was founded in 1928 by Dr. Bernard Revel in New York City (see Ch. 48). At that time pooling together dreams and means, there was erected at the cost of $2,500,000 a building on Amsterdam Avenue and 187th Street in Washington Heights.

In September of that year, the college reopened its doors with a small full house; only forty and so undergraduates arose one autumn

Yeshiva College

In September of that year the college opened its doors with a small full-time faculty and a distinguished associated faculty, consisting of eminent Jewish and Gentile professors. The authority to offer courses leading to the degrees of Bachelor of Arts and Bachelor of Science was conferred upon it.

The student body was required to attend simultaneously either the Rabbi Isaac Elchanan Theological Seminary preparing students for the rabbinate or the Teachers' Institute, for a full program of Jewish studies in addition to the college program. Since it was intended that Jewish education should be in addition to, and not in the place of a thorough college program of liberal studies, little credit, only two points a semester of the one hundred and twenty-eight required for graduation, was allowed for the requirements for the Bachelor's degree.

In September 1932, the first number of "Scripta Mathematica," a quarterly journal devoted to philosophy, history, and expository treatment of mathematics appeared. Subsequently, two other publications were launched. Honorary degrees which the institution had been authorized to grant have been conferred upon Dr. John Finley, at one time editor of the "The New York Times"; Herbert Lehman; Albert Einstein; Justice Benjamin Cardozo (see Ch. 78); Dr. Frank Graves, then New York State Commissioner of Education and others.

In 1945 the New York State Board of Regents conferred university rank upon the Yeshiva and it became the first sectarian American university under Jewish auspices. In 1950 the same body granted the Yeshiva a Charter permitting the establishment of a Medical School. This will mark the first Medical School under Jewish auspices in the entire history of Diaspora Jewry.

Today the buildings of Yeshiva University spread over two city blocks and fifteen hundreds students from all parts of the world are enrolled in its eight schools.

From the beginning Yeshiva College graduates were prominent in service to Jewry, America and mankind as they are today.

84. THE FIRST INTRODUCTION OF HEBREW
IN THE PUBLIC SCHOOL CURRICULUM

The renaissance of the Hebrew language, like the creation of the Jewish State, has been one of the miracles of the twentieth century. The movement for the recognition of Hebrew as the language of the Jewish people has grown and taken root in the perception of conscious Jews everywhere.

Although the history of the study of Hebrew in this country goes back to the colonial era, when the first universities to be founded taught Hebrew as one of their subjects, it was not until 1929 that Hebrew was officially introduced into the public high school curriculum. In that year, the New York City Board of Education, not certain of the response of the students, introduced it as an experiment in two high schools which had a majority of Jewish students. The first ninety-five boys and girls who were admitted to the classes were warned that they might not receive any credit for Hebrew. There were no up-to-date books and few qualified teachers. However, with the help of organizations devoted to the development of Jewish education, these needs were supplied. The experiment proved successful. In 1932, Hebrew was officially adopted as a study on a par with all other modern languages.

The success of this project has helped to raise the dignity and morale of the Jewish youth of New York. The Jewish group has also been given an opportunity to teach and spread the living Hebrew language and through it the values of Hebrew civilization.

The study of Hebrew grew rapidly in popularity so that today it is now taught in thirty-eight high schools, ten junior high schools and two evening high schools. It is given as an elective, the same as any other language, with high school, regents and college entrance credit. It is to be expected that the splendid example set by the high schools of New York will be followed by other schools throughout the country.

It was in speaking of Hebrew in the public high schools of New York that Superintendent of Schools William Jansen made the following remarks:

"In a complex city like ours, one of the best ways for us
to get the kind of human relationships that we want, is
for us to understand the cultural backgrounds of the various
peoples who make up America. Much has been done recently to spread a knowledge of Hebrew Culture. To that
extent it has helped New Yorkers and people in the United
States generally, to live happier and more peacefully together."

85. THE FIRST AMERICAN JEWISH WOMAN
TO DIE IN BATTLE

Never before in the history of America have Jews risen to
the ranks they attained in the Second World War. At least
sixteen Jews were generals or admirals. More than ten thousand
were decorated for heroic action. More than 600,000 Jews, men,
and for the first time in America history, women, fought on the
various fronts of the war. They served their country in every
branch of the service — in the air, on the land and on the
sea. From Sergeant Meyer Levin to Major General Maurice
Rose, Jews in the lowliest to the highest ranks made the supreme
sacrifice for a country whose basic principles are so consistent
with the ideals of their religious faith.

The first American Army nurse killed on the Western Front
was Lieutenant Frances Y. Slanger, a Boston Jewish girl, who
died of wounds received in Belgium. In less than five weeks,
Miss Slanger, who had been stationed near the thickest of the
fighting, had cared for over 3,000 men. From the day she
waded ashore on Normandy and helped set up a field hospital,
to the last four months she spent in a front line tent, she grew
to love the American soldier for his gallantry, courage, and
sportsmanship. At two o'clock in the morning just before she
was killed, she wrote a letter to the "Stars and Stripes" pouring
forth her sensitive love, devotion, and admiration for the
American soldier. The letter was printed by the "Stars and
Stripes" fourteen days later and magnificently symbolizes the

noble, womanly, American and Jewish qualities, of Nurse Frances Y. Slanger of blessed memory.

The B'nai B'rith have contributed $2,000 to the nation wide campaign for the erection of a national Nurses Memorial Home in Washington, D. C., in memory of the nurses who lost their lives in the war and where Americans for generations to come may learn to know of Lieutenant Slanger, and honor her and her kind.

86.   THE FIRST ARMY COMMANDER SINCE NAPOLEON TO INVADE THE REICH

Major General Maurice Rose of Denver, Colorado, who helped liberate Belgium, was the first army commander since Napoleon to invade the Reich from the west.

The son of a ninety year old Denver rabbi, he was named "one of America's greatest soldiers." After leading a brilliant campaign, he died in combat on March 30, 1945. "Although Major General Maurice Rose's body reached Padderton on a litter atop the hood of a jeep, his spirit and brain had enabled the Third Armored Division to accomplish one of the greatest surprise dashes in all military history."

With the enemy army slaughtered or captured, General Rose, who had taken over the Third Armored several weeks before, made a quick turn northeastward and during the next eight days helped to liberate Belgium. The victorious Armored Command continued its spectacular campaign.

Thomas R. Henry who talked with General Rose shortly before his death writes: " . . But the tanks had been almost constantly on the move and in action for more than two months. The big steel machine was running on nerve and mechanical miracles. Tanks were tied together with bailing wire. The First Army was short of gasoline. The men had been pushed to the limit of human endurance."

There was a moonlight battle for the city of Marburg. .

This is recognized as one of the most crucial actions of the war. It is referred to in War Department reports as "the battle of the rose pocket" in memory of the leader who fell there. After that everything was anti-climax. The Third Armored continued Westward . . . it liberated the terrible prison camp of Nordhausen; . . . the men of the Third Armored found the bodies of slave workers in piles like corkwood.

Secretary of War Stimson eulogizing General Rose, described his death as a "severe loss", and said, "No one more skillful there was in directing the operations of an armored column"

More than ten thousand men of General Rose's division contributed thirty thousand dollars towards a million dollar hospital to be erected in Denver— and to be known as the General Maurice Rose Hospital.

87. THE FIRST ATOMIC WEAPONS

It has been previously stated that every American War has been marked by some new invention. The Civil War was the first in which the railroad was a significant factor. In the Spanish American War, the steam propelled navy ship was the outstanding thing. The First World War was the first in which the airplane was used. The Second World War was marked by the introduction of atomic weapons.

On October 11, 1939, a month and a day before the Pearl Harbor incident, Professor Albert Einstein, the greatest scientist alive today, sent a letter to President Franklin D. Roosevelt, pointing out that "the Germans are working on atomic fission and the United States must start research at once or civilization will perish."

The President began to act. The United States Government's program on atomic research was set in motion, and four billion dollars of the American taxpayers money was risked on the Manhattan project. An advisory committee on uranium was promptly appointed. Research was carried on simultaneously in many American universities. The most significant development was the first successful atomic "chain reaction pile" achieved on the squash courts of the University of Chicago.

Albert Einstein

Meanwhile, the United States atomic power development program at the Los Alamos, New Mexico branch of the Manhattan project, was placed under the direction of Prof. J. Robert Oppenheimer, a forty-one year old Jewish physicist.

At 5:30 A.M. on July 16, 1945, the skies over the desert lands of New Mexico were rent by a terrifying explosion. Its dazzling burst of light was brighter than the noon day sun; its heat melted the desert sand and rocks and flowed them together. A great volcano of dust and debris churned from the desert and seethed high into the sky.

The group of scientists assigned to the Los Alamos branch, working on Einstein's equation of the conversion of matter into energy and the uranium fission theory evolved by Niels Bohr, Jewish physicist and Nobel Prize winner from Denmark, and his Jewish colleague, Lisa Meitner, were enabled to make the atom bomb. Their experimental bomb— perhaps the most important single experiment ever attempted by man— was a success. The key to the release of the almost limitless power within the atom had been found. Man had entered the age of atomic energy.

The first atom bomb to be used in warfare was dropped on Hiroshima, Japan on August 5, 1945. More than four square miles, 60 percent of Hiroshema was blown off the face of the earth.

Mankind is now faced with the greatest challenge of all time. Will we use this power to blast civilization from the earth, or will we learn to apply it usefully in all fields of endeavor in a world where each of us is the next door neighbor to everyone else?

88.   THE FIRST NATIONAL SHRINE OF JUDAISM
IN AMERICA

Among the first of Newport, Rhode Island's settlers, were Jews who could find freedom of worship in no other place. Most of their fathers and mothers and some of them, had fled religious persecution in the old world and had found respite

Interior of Touro Synagogue

and a new home in this newest of lands— America. For over a hundred years now they had lived in freedom and in tolerance in this land and had worshipped God in their own fashion— in the same manner as had Abraham and all his seed. The members of the Jewish community had prospered in the new land and now they decided to build a new temple to praise the Almighty. One of the finest architects of the day, Peter Harrison, was called in to design the synagogue. (see Ch. 16). In 1760, bricks were imported from abroad and the building began. Finally, in 1763, the synagogue of the "Jeshuat Israel Congregation" was dedicated. Rabbi Isaac Touro, an immigrant from Holland was asked to be its first rabbi. He led the congregation until 1780, when the Revolutionary War caused the temporary closing of its doors. Rabbi Touro left Newport and went to New York to act as the rabbi for the "Shearith Israel Congregation." Later, he migrated to the West Indian Island of Kingston in Jamaica where he died.

Many members of the congregation took part in our nation's early struggle for liberty. They included soldiers, business men, financiers, and such patriots as Aaron Lopez who sacrificed his personal fortune to further the America cause. When the two sons of Rabbi Touro died, Abraham in 1822 and Judah in 1854, each left liberal provisions in his will for the care and the preservation of the synagogue and the surrounding cemetery. (see Ch. 39).

The Touro Synagogue, so called after its first rabbi, a splendid example of colonial architecture and clothed with historic associations has been carefully preserved. Like a little treasure island among the colonial buildings that surround it, it still stands in perfect condition after hundreds of years. Its woodwork is all hand carved. The masonic plan of the structure follows the Temple of Jerusalem. Twelve columns represent the twelve tribes of Israel, each being made of a solid tree trunk. No metal has been used in the building, every unit having been joined by dovetail and wood pin. Among objects of beautifully wrought silver still in existance today is a great center candelabrum.

In 1946, the Government of the United States, recognizing

the fact that the synagogue had lived the history of the country and survived as the oldest synagogue building in America, designated the Touro Synagogue a national historic site, the first national shrine of Judaism in this country.

Although the National Park Service of the Department of the Interior aids in caring for the synagogue, the ownership of the building remains with "Shearith Israel" of New York which became guardian of the ancient structure and its burying grounds where so many of the ancestors of its early members had worshipped and were buried after Newport lost its high standing following the Revolution. During the past forty years Jews began to filter back to Newport and today the "Congregation Jeshuat Israel" continues to be used as a place of worship. In connection with its dedication as a national shrine, there has been incorporated the Society of the Friends of Touro National Historic Shrine.

89.   THE FIRST TO RECEIVE
THE JEWISH WAR VETERANS ORDER OF MERIT AWARD

The first Order of Merit ever awarded by the Jewish War Veterans of the United States was presented in 1947 to Bernard Baruch, America's "unofficial president" and oft-hailed "apostle of peace."

Embodied in bronze, plaque, the order cited Mr. Baruch as an outstanding citizen and "the world's foremost humanitarian."

That this honor should be bestowed upon Mr. Baruch is not unusual. A faithful servant of the American people through the regime of six presidents from Woodrow Wilson to Harry S. Truman, his unselfish deeds have made him a living American legend. During America's two great wars of survival, he was the one individual, though not an official of any government agency, called upon to help solve a nation's crisis. When peacetime problems supplemented those of war, President Truman summoned Baruch to help work out a way of life for

the American people. Heralded as America's "elder statesman", he is still an individual whose advice is eagerly sought
after by all the important Washington agencies.

Baruch's career is unlike that of other prominent Jews in
that he did not have to start from scratch in carving out his
empire. His mother who was of Spanish-Portuguese extraction,
and his father of German-Jewish descent, had wealth to start
with. At the age of eleven he moved with his family from
his birth-place Camden, South Carolina, where his father had
been a prominent Civil War surgeon, to New York. After
graduation from City College, he got his start as a clerk in the
brokerage firm of A. Houseman at three dollars a week. A few
years later he worked his way into the partnership of the firm
where he acquired the basis for his world-famous stockmarket
techniques. At the age of thirty, he became know as America's
most fascinating financier and was making and losing fortunes.

Before, during and after World War I, he led nine government posts under Presidents Wilson and Harding, including the
War Industries Board. It was his "know how" in this capacity
that enabled America to defeat Kaiser Wihelm. In World War
II, whether it was the broad problems of defense, the rubber
shortage, the manpower squeeze, lagging war plane production,
or factory reconversion, President Roosevelt summoned this man
of facts to devise escape from the bewildering tangle.

In 1946 upon reaching the three score and ten mark, for
nine long months he began the most important job of his career. As United States representative on the Atomic Energy
Commission of the United Nations, Mr. Baruch grapled with
the most dreaded and mightiest force man had ever unleashed,
atomic power. In lauding the "elder statesman's" tireless and
patriotic endeavors on behalf of atomic control, President
Truman asserted that the prevention of atomic war was a
tribute to Baruch's patience and skill.

It was precisely because of his profound faith in moral values
and basic human decencies that Mr. Baruch chided the nations of the world, including our own, for their lack of moral
watchfulness in approaching the Jewish problem, and admis-

sion of Jewish refugees in Israel. Despite his hard work, he has kept a watchful eye on what is going on in Europe and rose to almost prophetic heights when he told an audience early in 1950 that "politics of a dubious nature had swayed the world from the plainly marked path of duty."

Yet while in the midst of an atomic bomb controversy which itself reflects and epitomizes the moral decline of man, Mr. Baruch had faith to assert that "the moral side of the Palestine and refugee question had been ignored and wiped out," thus presupposing the existence of moral factors and considereration in international and human relations.

90. THE FIRST AMERICAN POSTAGE STAMP BEARING THE PICTURE OF A JEW

In 1947 to commemorate the one hundredth anniversary of the birth of Joseph Pulitzer, founder of "The New York World" and father of the flaming headline, the United States Post Office issued a special stamp bearing his picture. The "World's" editorial page written by Pulitzer was considered the best in the country by many serious students of journalism and it was from him that William Randolph Hearst learned his journalistic tactics.

Pulitzer was born in Budapest, Hungary in 1847, the son of a Hungarian-Jewish father and an Austro-German mother. At the age of seventeen he ran away from his home in Budapest and signed up with a recruiting agent in Hamburg, Germany, to fight on the Northern side in the American Civil War. When his ship reached Boston Harbor he jumped off and swam ashore to collect his own bounty for enlisting. After the war he made his way to St. Louis and got a job as a reporter on a German-language newspaper, the "Westliche Post." On December 9, 1878, the dying "St. Louis Dispatch," an evening newspaper with practically no assets, was offered at auction. Pulitzer, who had made some money by buying and selling an interest in the "Westliche Post", bid $2,500 and was handed the paper. The next day he formed a partnership with the evening "Post", and on December 12 the first issue of the "Post-Dispatch" was published. Today its plants and goodwill are valued at more than $10,000,000 and its earnings have often exceeded $1,000,000 a year.

After four years of his lively editorialship the "Post Dispatch" was earning Pulitzer $85,000 a year. But the hard work had impaired his health and eyesight. Stopping off on his way to a rest in Europe in 1883, in New York, he learned that, "The New York World" was for sale. He bought it and buckled down again to the process of newspaper-building on an even bigger scale. In a relatively few years he had converted, "The New York World" into one of the most popular and profitable papers of all time, but the efforts left him totally blind and a chronic invalid. From 1890 until the time of his death in 1911, he lived mostly on his yacht, where his six secretaries read to him or jotted down his continuous flow of instructions to his newspapers.

He was the first one to conceive the idea of establishing a School of Journalism at Columbia and founded a number of scholarships which included the Pulitzer Prize, the highest award that a paper, writer or original American play can win.

91. THE FIRST ORIGINAL DOCUMENT BY A JEWISH AUTHOR ON THE NEW YORK STATE FREEDOM TRAIN

The most significant piece of paper which has become an emblem of American humanity towards all refugees from persecution and horror has been included among New York State's Freedom Train's exhibitions. Borrowed from its shrine in the archives of the American Jewish Historical Society, from the original manuscript autograph notebook of the poems of Emma Lazarus, "The New Colossus" has been on display in New York State. Thousands of its citizens gazed in reverence on the original document, in ink that has faded these seventy-five years, but in words that never dim:

"Send these, the homeless, the tempest tossed to me!
I lift my lamp beside the Golden Door!"
These words will live when all her other poems are forgotten. They will tell the world the story of Emma Lazarus who returned to her people.

A hundred years ago, a little dark-eyed girl was growing up in the comfortable home of her Sephardic parents in New York. Though her private tutors taught little Emma classic literature and modern language, none seemed to acquaint the gifted child with the glorious past and present of her people. As she matured her close friend, Ralph Waldo Emerson, praised highly Emma's early poems about Greek legends. Basking in the glow of such praise, Emma continued to pursue her "calm hellenism" ideals of beauty. In 1879, she was suddenly brought to a rude awakening of her Jewish soul. The papers blazed the awful tidings of Russian persecutions. A great wave of immigrants was hurled at the shores of the New World. Emma Lazarus saw them in Wards Island; she saw their poverty and distress, but also their pride and devotion to their ancient faith. From then on she seemed to be reborn for the rest of her all too short life, and belonged like one of her heroines termed it "wholly to her people." She learned Hebrew and translated some of the finest medieval poets, Ibon Gabirol, Judah Halevi and others. Long before Zionism had become a contemporary force, she became the first to appeal for funds to colonize Jews in Palestine. Full of sympathy for the persecuted, she rose to attack the dark forces of persecution, and found the words that were to create for her a niche for all time among the American immortals.

In 1883 when a fund was being raised for the pedestal of the Statue of Liberty presented by France, Miss Lazarus contributed her poem "The New Colossus", a fourteen line sonnet, that depicted America as the home of the oppressed. Its benefits sale brought an unheard of amount for a short piece of poetry: $1,500. The verses went from mouth to mouth, from continent to continent, and in 1903 they were inscribed in a plaque placed on the base of the statue.

The "Goddess of Liberty" and Emma Lazarus have become

synonymous; few poets of all nations and all times have achieved such distinction. As long as the Statue of Liberty will remain the symbol of American Freedom, the name of Emma Lazarus will be associated with that symbol as the champion of liberty.

92. THE FIRST AMERICAN JEW TO GIVE HIS LIFE FOR THE STATE OF ISRAEL

At 4 o'clock on the afternoon of May 14, 1948, David Ben-Gurion read to a small audience in the Museum of Art in Tel Aviv: "We. . .hereby proclaim the establishment of the Jewish State in Palestine, to be called Israel."

After centuries of persecution and wandering, after inhuman suffering and superhuman sacrifice, the ancient hope is fulfilled. A people breathes the air of a free land, a land where it can be itself once more.

It is a strange thing. The men of the American Revolution proclaimed the doctrine "that resistance to tyranny is obedience to doctrine." These Founding Fathers of America found inspiration in the Bible story of the Jews in ancient Palestine (see Ch. 18). In our own day, the Jews of Palestine found inspiration for their struggle in the story of the founding of America and of the fight which was necessary to attain its liberty. In Palestine, the Jews showed that they were willing to give unstinted of "their lives, fortunes and sacred honor" as our own Declaration of Independence puts it.

American Jews who had just put off their uniforms following World War II could not stand idly by. They could not read of the heartless condition of the suffering Jews of the displaced persons camps, or of a tyranny which exposed itself to the world as one whose word and solemn promise could not be trusted from day to day. They had not fought a war for such a solution.

Dov Seligman, formerly of 1565 Grand Concourse, the Bronx, New York, was one of the many young Americans who went from uniform to uniform. Their war was somehow not to be

counted finished until the last displaced person was provided
with an address. In January 1942, Dov, a two hundred pound
six footer, enlisted in the United States Army. In 1944 he was
sent to the Pacific Theatre of the war as a sergeant in the ground
crew of an air transport command unit. In 1946 he was mus-
tered out and promptly transferred himself to Palestine in a
settlement owned and operated by the Shomer Hatzir, a Zionist youth organization. While driving a tractor on the collec-
tive settlement, he was ambushed by Arabs and killed early in
1948. This announcement followed by two days the disclosure
that another American, Moshe Pearlstein, a Brooklyn youth had
been slain by Arabs in the Holy Land, while leading a food
convey to a settlement of the Hapoel Hamizrachi.

October 10, 1948 was set aside to honor another fallen Brooklyn hero. It was called "Colonel Marcus Day" in memory of
Colonel David Marcus, a veteran of World War II who was
killed on June 10, while leading Israeli troops near Jerusalem.
He was at the time supreme commander of the Jewish forces
in Jerusalem. A graduate of West Point, he was formerly New
York City Commissioner of Correction. The perfect accolade
for this hero and his comrads in arms came from President
Truman who wrote that the life and death of Colonel Marcus "symbolizes all that is best in the unending struggle for
liberty."

93. THE FIRST ISRAELI AMBASSADOR TO AMERICA

When the Jewish State was proclaimed on May 14, 1948,
Eliahu Elath, was named the first official diplomatic representative of Israel in the United States.

Elath's first direct contact with United States officials was
made at the San Francisco Conference, and this helped pave
the way for him subsequently in Washington and as advisor to
the Jewish Agency delegation at Lake Success when the Parti-
tion of Palestine was under discussion. With the exception of
brief visits to Palestine and as a delegate to the World Zionist
Congress at Basle in December, 1946, Elath served continu-

ously in Washington as the Agency's representative and director of its office. Here he worked with a small staff, including several Palestinians, who helped him in his day to day work.

Still a young man for his accomplishments, Elath was born in the town of Snovsk, in the Ukraine on September 16, 1904. He received a good Jewish education and at the age of seventeen entered the University of Kiev. At the age of twenty-one, he left Soviet Russia, and worked for two years in the fields of Palestine, and continued his studies at the Hebrew University. Moving to neighboring Transjordan, he lived among the native Arab population, observed Bedouin life and customs, and studied the Arabic language. In 1930 he was granted a scholarship by the Rockefeller Foundation to continue his studies on Arabic civilization at the American University in Beirut, Lebanon. The result of these studies was two volumes which he published in Hebrew: "The Bedouins, Their Life and Their Customs" and "The Population of Transjordan." In addition, he also published many articles and studies dealing with the social conditions of the native population in Lebanon, Transjordan, and other Near Eastern Countries.

Back home, his knowledge of Arab affairs was soon recognized and he was taken on by the Jewish Agency as its Arab expert. As director of the Jewish Agency's Washington office, he worked tirelessly to obtain approval of a Jewish State. It was he who wrote President Truman the memorandum requesting that the United States extend full recognition to the new State. It was he, also, who was the first one to be informed by President Truman that the United States had granted recognition to the Jewish State.

Soon after Mr. Elath's appointment in 1948, Mr. James G. McDonald was chosen the first United States Ambassador to Israel. Mr. McDonald, a political scientist who became deeply involved in the refugee problem has been intimately associated with Jewish affairs over the past quarter century. As an expert on displaced persons, he was a logical choice for membership on the Anglo-American Committee of Inquiry on Palestine, and became well known for his sympathy for the Zionist cause in the developing struggle for the independent Jewish state. When Mr. McDonald as ambassador arrived in Israel he

The Hon. Eliahu Elath

came as a warm personal friend of many people who were now the leaders in the Israeli government.

In 1950 there appeared the book "My Mission in Israel", the frank, personal report of America's first ambassador to Israel.

94.   THE FIRST WOMAN RABBI IN AMERICA

The list of Jewish women who have made contributions to the development of the Jewish people and to the cause of humanity is a long and glorious one. In secular life they have distinguished themselves in music, acting, embroidery painting and have entered the legal, medical and teaching professions.

With one exception in Great Britain where for the past fifteen years Mrs. Lily Montague of London has been acting as spiritual leader of a Reform Jewish congregation, an exceptional historic making event in the world-wide practice of Judaism since the days of Abraham, occurred in America in 1950, with the appointment of a woman rabbi to serve as spiritual leader of a Jewish congregation.

The woman rabbi is Mrs. William Ackerman, widow of the late rabbi of Temple Beth Israel of Meridian, Mississippi. Although Mrs. Ackerman lacks official ordination from a recognized rabbinical school, a requisite of both Orthodox and Conservative Judaism, her succession to the post of her husband was made possible by a recent ruling in Reform Judaism. She has the full powers of a rabbi and the state of Mississippi has given her permission to perform marriages.

Mrs. Ackerman at the time of her appointment was fifty-seven years old and had had a lifetime of experience as a rabbi's wife in attending the affairs of a congregation. As such she is a manager, a psychologist, a preacher, a teacher, and has learned much in having to deal directly with human beings all her life. Her appointment is unique and may open a new channel of special appeal to spiritual women whose preachments to date have been limited to families and friends.

Throughout the ages, Jewish women have manifested more than their share of humanitarianism and scholarship. Prior to

Mrs. Ackerman's appointment, the nearest to an orthodox woman rabbi in our own country is Dr. Trude Weiss Rosmarin, editor of "The Jewish Spectator" and author of several books, though she is without a pulpit or congregation.

Today more than ever, American women can rise to the stature of an Isaiah or a Hulda, if they answer the call within their own hearts to build a better world.

95. THE FIRST JEWISH WOMAN MAYOR IN AMERICA

Mrs. Katherine Elkus White, in the November 1950 elections, scored three firsts — one for the Jewish people, one for the female sex, and one for the Democratic Party — by winning the mayoralty election in the city of Red Bank, New Jersey.

She is not only the first woman in our history to be mayor of this American city, but also the first Jewish woman to hold this post. Her victory is even a greater feat since she won the office on the Democratic ticket in a very strong Republican stronghold. The record further shows that she is the first Democratic mayor of Red Bank in the past twenty years.

Mrs. White, a forty-four year old housewife and mother of two children, is the daughter of Abram J. Elkus, one-time United States Ambassador to Turkey and a judge of the United States Court of Appeals. Mayor White's father was prominent in Jewish affairs and a man of determination.

Mrs. White showed that same grit in capturing the office of mayor. She spoke before dozens of civic groups to get her platform across—especially in encouragement of Red Bank's youth in useful activities; an adequate civil defense program; an increase in the local tax rate and other matters.

Active in numerous civic and other organizations, a member of the local unit of Hadassah, the Women's Zionist Organization, Mrs. White believes that the Average Mr. Citizen opens up more quickly in his problems and cares to a woman mayor than a male mayor. In her short opening days as mayor of Red Bank, dozens of citizens put in appearances at City Hall. Many of their problems were of a personal nature, but Mrs. White, believing that any problems, personal or otherwise, confronting Red Bank's citizens are of prime importance to the community, and listened patiently as residents sought — and obtained — her assistance.

America's first Jewish woman mayor who squeezed into office in one of this North New Jersey community's closest elections — a plurality of a bare sixty-five votes, is especially popular among the young generation. Sharing her day between tending house and City Hall, Mrs. White is doing Red Bank a great deal of good. The residents of the community are all behind her.

96. THE FIRST JEWISH WOMAN IN AMERICA TO OCCUPY A HIGH FEDERAL POST

American Jews have recognized that the equality of all citizens under the American constitution imposes civic duties and responsibilities. They have taken part in municipal, state, and national affairs. In 1950, for the first time in American history, a Jewish woman, Mrs. Anna M. Rosenberg was appointed to the high public office of Assistant Secretary of Defense, in charge of directing the mobilization of American manpower.

Known widely in the past for her skill in dealing with troubled labor relations, Mrs. Rosenberg who was summoned at the request of Secretary of War George C. Marshall, now presides firmly if not placidly, in what is probably the most important public task entrusted to any woman in American history.

"Aunt Anna" as she is affectionately called in Pentagon circles, knows her business, and learned from experience with life and practical affairs. She was a wife at eighteen, a mother at twenty, and in business as a labor consultant at twenty-three. In the late 1920's she was dubbed the busiest woman in New York. Since then she has maintained her own consultant office in New York and held some twenty-five government jobs, all of which have earned her a Master's degree in Humane Letters, a Medal of Freedom from General Eisenhower and a Medal of Merit from President Truman.

Anna Rosenberg entered manpower problems while still in

high school. A junior in Wadleigh High School for Girls in New York City, at the outbreak of World War I, she took a personal interest in the fight against Prussian militarism. She served as a volunteer nurse at a debarkation hospital and sold Liberty Bonds. One week her street corner sales totaled $2,850 in thrift stamps and $5,700 in bonds. It was here too, that she settled her first strike. When two thousand students went out in strike against military drill during hours they considered undesirable, she called a meeting and talked the strikers into cooperating with the school authorities.

Mrs. Rosenberg personifies what used to be called the American ideal. A self-made woman, foreign born, who was driven from Hungary at the age of ten, she carved out for herself such a position that large corporations paid huge sums for her advice, and leaders of America are proud to be her friends. When she was attacked by anti-Semitism, and the baseness of the attacks were exposed, the little forty-nine year old Jewish woman of the Pentagon was vindicated and applauded as was her due.

97. THE FIRST AMERICAN ACTOR TO BE AWARDED A DOCTOR'S DEGREE

Eddie Cantor, America's widely beloved screen star, who was awarded the degree of Doctor of Humane Letters on June 14, 1951, at Temple University, is the first actor in America to rate the degree.

Born in 1893 on New York's Lower East Side with all the cards stacked against him, he grew up to be a highly rated screen, stage, and television comedian, philanthropist, model husband and father.

Cantor made his "professional" debut at amateur night at Miner's Bowery Theater at the age of eighteen. Continuing his "career" he joined a burlesque show as singing waiter in Coney Island. His first real break came in 1912 when he joined Gus Edwards' "Kid Kabaret" along with George Jessel and Walter Winchell who was then a dancer. A good part in his first musical

Eddie Cantor

comedy quickly followed as did an offer from the fabulous Florenz Ziegfeld to appear in the "Midnight Frolics," and his marriage to Ida. Soon came "Broadway Brevities" in 1920, "Make It Snappy" in 1922, and stardom in "Kid Boots" in 1923. Reaching the top, he made many movies including such hits as "Whoopee," "Kid From Spain," "Roman Scandals," and "Strike Me Pink," and later entered radio. Besides entertaining millions, he introduced such stars as Deanna Durbin, Dinah Shore and George Burns and Gracie Allen.

Despite his rise to face, Eddie Cantor never forgot the underprivileged youth. In the early 1930's he financed a camp in New York for underprivileged and impoverished children. When Hitler came to power, he conducted an intensive tour of England and the United States to raise funds for Youth Aliyah so that refugee children could escape to Israel. He brought in close to a million dollars. In 1936 he originated the "March of Dimes." Donating to numerous charities and working for better inter-cultural relations, he has spent almost as much time in welfare work during the past decade as in being an entertainer.

His well-earned doctorate citation appropriately reads:

"A great American, endowed with high personal ideals and generosity of spirit, whose innate talents as entertainer have made him a national institution . . . His great use of his life is to spend it for something that outlasts life itself, for his humane activities in bringing pleasure to mankind do not end at the footlights or before the cameras."

98. THE FIRST SABBATH OBSERVING RETAIL CHAIN IN AMERICA

The Sabbath, in Jewish tradition and history, occupies a preeminent position. It has nurtured the intellect as well as the soul of the Jew; it has counterbalanced his disappointments; and it has afforded him a blessed opportunity for personality adjustments.

Under the impact of the tensions of our technological age, the observance of the Sabbath has tragically suffered. Because of the pressures of economic necessity, many an American Jew has been deprived of experiencing the delights of the Sabbath; he has even spurned often those Sabbath delights which he could experience.

The keen competitive business life of a driving metropolis as New York would at first discourage the most stalwart from ever considering the closing of his business on the Sabbath. This would especially affect a retail store which statistically speaking does a major part of its business on the Sabbath. Until recently, this conviction was so strong that it was an almost impossible task to convince one to keep his retail business closed on the Sabbath. With the establishment of the Barton Candy Chain starting with one store in 1940 to its present number of forty-nine throughout metropolitan New York, New Jersey and Detroit, for the first time in American history, it became much easier to show the people that "it can be done." Now for the first time a tremendous chain of stores and a factory employing over one thousand people closed for the holiness of the Sabbath as well as all Jewish holidays and still remains as one of the leaders in the business field.

Another milestone in the living example of the possibility of Sabbath observance was set behind the opening in April of 1951 of Barton's subway store at New York's IRT Grand Central end of the shuttle train. Here lies the story of the first recognition of Jewish Sabbath observance by the New York City Board of Transportation. At the time bids were submitted by various companies for this retail space. Considerable pressure was brought to bear on the city not to award the bid to Barton's because of Barton's Sabbath closing policy, which was claimed "would diminish the city's returns."

The Board of Transportation noted that all of the stores operated by Barton's were closed from sunset on Friday to nightfall, on Saturday, for the observance of the Sabbath of the Jewish faith. If the contract were awarded to Barton's this location "would also be operated in conformity with the policy of the company."

After hearing the evidence submitted by the competing companies, the Board of Transportation decided that Barton's Sabbath observing policy would not "affect the revenue to be derived from this location," and awarded the contract to Barton's.

Much of the success of the Barton chain can be accredited to its president and founder, Mr. Stephen Klein, who in the face of strong pressure groups outside of his organizations, and even against the advice of many so-called business experts, instituted and retained his Sabbath observing policy.

The Barton chain can also claim several other "firsts." It is the first American firm to use Jewish history and tradition as a source material for packaging. It is the first and only one to include in its candy boxes educational and play material on the Jewish holidays. Its cartoon technique which tells the story of the various Jewish holidays is being used by Jewish religious schools throughout the country, as it meets with the best educational requirements.

BIBLIOGRAPHY

Adams, James Truslow, Album of American History, 3 vols. New York, 1944-6.

————, The Founding of New England. Boston, 1927.

Adler, Cyrus, Jacob H. Schiff, His Life and Letters, 2 vols. New York, 1928

————, "Adolphus Simeon Solomons and the Red Cross, "P.A.J.H.S.*, XXXII, New York, 1934.

————, "Oscar S. Straus", American Jewish Yearbook, New York, 5688.

Arnold, Samuel Greene, History of the State of Rhode Island and Providence Plantations, 2 vols. Providence, 1894.

Bigelow, Bruch M., "Aaron Lopez, Merchant of Newport," The New England Quarterly, IV, no. 4. Portland, Me., 1931.

Bishop, John Leander, History of American Manufacturing, Philadelphia, 1861.

Brodhead, John Romeyn, History of the State of New York, 2 vols. New York, 1853-1871.

Bloom, Herbert I., "A study of Brazilian Jewish History, 1623-1654, Based Chiefly upon the Findings of the Late Samuel Oppenheim," P. A. J. H. S., XXXIII. New York, 1934.

Channing, Edward A., History of the United States, 6 vols. New York, 1905-1925.

Daly, Charles P., The Settlement of the Jews in North America. New York, 1893.

Dexter, Franklin B., Literary Diary of Ezra Stiles, New York, 1901.

Documents Relating to the Colonial History of the State of New York, 15 vols., Albany, 1853-1887.

Drayton, John, Memoirs of the American Revolution. 2 vols. Charleston, 1821.

Fernow, Berthold, ed., The Records of New Amsterdam from 1653 to 1674, Anno Domini, 7 vols. New York, 1902-1907.

Fredman, George and Falk, Louis, Jews in American Wars, New York, 1942.

* Publications of the American Jewish Historical Society.

Friedman, Lee M., Early American Jews, Cambridge, 1934.
————, Jewish Pioneers and Patriots, Phila., 1942.
————, Pilgrims in a New Land, Philadelphia, 1948.
————, "Judah Monis, First Instructor of Hebrew at Harvard Univer." P.A.J.H.S., XII. N.Y. 1914.
Goldberg, Isaac Major Noah; American-Jewish Pioneer. Philadelphia, 1936.
Goodman, Abram V., American Overture, Phila., 1947.
Grinstein, Hyman B, The Rise of the Jewish Community of New York, 1654-1860, Philadelphia, 1947.
Gutstein, Morris A., The Story of the Jews of Newport. New York, 1936.
Hower, Ralph M., The History of Macy's. Cambridge, 1943.
Huhner, Leon, "Asser Levy: A Noted Jewish Burgher of New Amsterdam," P.A.J.H.S., VIII. N.Y., 1905.
————, "Francis Salvador, a Prominent Patriot of the Revolutionary War," P.A.J.H.S., IX. New York 1901.
————, "Jews in Connection with Colleges of the Thirteen Original States Prior to 1800," P.A.J.H.S., XIX. New York, 1902.
————, "The First Jew to Hold the Office of Governor of One of the United States," P.A.J.H.S., XVII. New York, 1909.
————, "The Jews of South Carolina from the Earliest Settlement to the End of the American Revolution," P.A.J.H.S., XII. New York, 1904.
Janvier, Thomas A., In Old New York, 1894.
Johnston, Mary, Pioneers of the Old South, New Haven, 1918.
Johnson, Melvin M., The Beginnings of Freemansonry in America, Washington, 1924.
Kagan, Solomon R., Contributions of Early Jews to American Medicine. Boston, 1934.
Kayserling, Meyer, Christopher Columbus and the Participation of the Jews in the Spanish and Portuguese Discoveries. New York, 1894.
Kohler, Max J., "Beginnings of New York Jewish History, P.A.J.H.S., I. New York, 1893.

————, "Civil Status of the Jews in Colonial New York," P.A.J.H.S., VI. New York 1897.

————, "Phases of Jewish Life in New York Before 1800," P.A.J.H.S., III. New York, 1895.

————, "The Jews of Newport," P.A.J.H.S., VI. New York, 1897.

————, "Haym Salomon, the Patriot Broker of the Revolution—His Real Achievements and Their Exaggeration." Privately Printed.

Korn, Harold, "Documents Relative to the Estate of Aaron Lopez," P.A.J.H.S., XXXV. New York, 1939.

Lebeson, Anita L., Jewish Pioneers in America. N. Y., 1931.

The Lyons Collections, P.A.J.H.S., XXI, XXVII. New York, 1913, 1920.

Makover, Abraham B., Mordecai M. Noah. New York, 1917.

Markens, Isaac, "Abraham Lincoln and the Jews," P.A.J. H.S., XXIX. New York, 1925.

————, The Hebrews in America. New York, 1888.

McCall, S.W., Patriotism of the American Jew. N.Y., 1924.

Mendes, Rev. A.P., "The Jewish Cemetery at Newport, Rhode Island," *The Rhode Island Historical Magazine*, VI, no. 2, Newport, Oct. 1885.

Morais, Henry S., Eminent Israelites of the Nineteenth Century. New York, 1924.

Morison, Samuel Eliot, Harvard College in the Seventeenth Century, 2 vols. Cambridge, 1936.

Newport Historical Society, Manuscript Papers.

O'Callaghan, E.B., The Documentary History of the State of New York, 4 vols. Albany, 1850-1856.

Oppenheimer, Francis J., Ezekiel Through Einstein. New York, 1940.

Peters, Madison Clinton, Justice to the Jew. N. Y., 1894.

————, "Haym Salomon. New York, 1911.

Philipson, David, Letters of Rebecca Gratz. Phila., 1929.

Phillips, Rosalie S., "A Burial Place for the Jewish Nation Forever," P.A.J.H.S., XVIII. New York, 1909.

Pool, Rev. David De Sola, "Hebrew Learning Among the Puritans of New England prior to 1700," P.A.J. H.S., XX. New York, 1911.

Proskauer, Bertha Richman, Julia Richman. N. Y., 1916.
Roth, Cecil, A History of the Marranos. Philadelphia, 1932.
————, Jewish Contributions to Civilization. Cincinnati, 1940.
Russell, Charles E., Haym Salomon and the Revolution. New York, 1930.
Rupp, Daniel, An Original History of the Religious Denominations in the United States. Phila., 1844.
Sacher, Abram L., "B'nai Brith Hillel Foundations,,' Universal Jewish Encyclopedia. II. New York, 1941.
Salley, Alexander S., Orginal Narratives of Reform Judaism. New York, 1905.
Sloane, William M., The French War and the Revolution. New York, 1901.
Soltes, Mordecai, The Yiddish Press as an Americanizing Agency. New York.
Starbuck, Alexander, History of the American Whale Industry. Waltham, 1878.
Straus, Oscar Solomon, Roger Williams, Pioneer of Religious Liberty. New York, 1894.
————, Origin of the Republican Form of Government. New York, 1901.
Thorowgood, Thomas, The Jew in America. London, 1664.
University of Pennsylvania, General Alumni Catalogue of the Philadelphia, 1917.
Webb, Mary, Famous Living Americans. Indiana, 1915.
Wiernik, Peter, History of the Jews in America. N.Y., 1912.
Wile, Frederck, Emile Berliner, Indianapolis, 1926.
Wise, James Waterman, Jews Are Like That. N. Y., 1928.
Wise, Stephen S. The Challenging Years; An Autobiography. Philadelphia, 1949.
Wolf, Simon. The Jew as Patriot, Soldier, and Citizen. New York, 1895.
Wolfson, Harry A., "Judah Monis," *Dictionary of American Biography*, XIII. New York, 1934.
Yeshiva *University*, General Catalogue of the. N.Y., 1950.
Zwierlein, Frederick J., Religion in New Netherland. Rochester, 1910.

INDEX

A. F. OF L., *see* AMERICAN FEDERA-
TION OF LABOR
Aaronsburg, Penn., 40, 41
Aboab, Isaac de Fonseca, 4
Abolitionists, 55
Abraham and Straus Department Store,
Brooklyn, N.Y., 95
Abravanel, Don Isaac, 1
Ackerman, Mrs. William, 149, 150
Act Concerning Religion, 16
Adams, Hannah, 56
Adams, John, 27
Adler, Dr. Cyrus, 55, 77, 83
Adler, Jacob, 102
Africa, 26
Agriculture, *see* International Institute
of Agriculture
Albany, N.Y., 57
Alexander, Gov. Moses, 122, 123
Ambassador, first from Israel, 147, 148,
149, 150
Ambrosius, Moses, 7
Amendment, the Nineteenth, 55
American Federation of Labor, 92
American Hebrew, the, 47
American Jewish Committee, 110, 114
American Jewish Congress, 117
American Jewish Historical Society,
14, 56, 57, 144
American Red Cross, 86, 87, 107
American Society for Ameliorating the
Condition of the Jews, 46, 56 *see
also* Missionary activities
American Revolution, 12, 13, 25, 26,
31, 40, 61, 64, 141, 146
American Tobacco Journal, the, 96
Amsterdam, 4, 6
Ami, Ben, 102
Anthony, Susan B., 55
Anti-Defamation League, 58
Anti-Semitism, 153
Arabian Nights, 42
Arabic language, 1, 149
Arabs, 147, 149
Ararat, Noah's proposed plan for, 49
Architecture of Touro Synagogue, 12

Arnold, General Benedict, 21
Arnold, Isaac N., 69
Artist, the first Jewish in America, 18,
19, 78, 79
Art, Jews in, 18, 19, 78, 79
Asmonean, The, 47
Asser Levy Garrison, the, 13
Astor, John Jacob, 23
Atom bomb, 138
Atomic weapons, the first, 136, 138
Atomic Energy Commission, 142
Attorney,General, United States, 37
Author, first Hebrew in America, 4, 5

BAER, CLARENCE, 126
Balfour Declaration, 112
Baltimore, Md., 47, 88
Bamberger, Gov. Simon, 122
Bank of North America, 37
Bar Mitzvah, 76
Barsimson, Jacob, 5, 6, 14
Barton's Candy Chain, 156, 157
Barton, Clara, 86
Baruch, Bernard M., 141, 142
Bay Psalm Book, 3
Bedside School, the first, 105
Belasco, David, 90, 91, 101
Belascoism, 90
Bell, Alexander Graham, 85
Bellevue Hospital, 64
Belgium, 135
Ben Gurion, David, 146
Benjamin, Judah P., 73, 74
Bennett, James Gordon, 49
Bernstein, Herman, 48
Bernal, Mastre, 1
Bes Sefer Yeshiva, 99
Beth Elohim Congregation, *see* Kahal
Kodesh Beth Elohim
Berlin, Hirsch Leib, 99
Berliner, Emile, 85, 86
Bible, the, 2, 3, 5, 8, 9, 18, 23, 27, 34,
42, 51, 56, 60, 61, 69, 103, 108, 114,
146